Rising to the Challenge

understanding
— A styles approach to ∧ adults with
ADD and other learning difficulties

D1707956

Dedicated to those who seek
understanding of learning differences

Rising to the Challenge

— A styles approach to *understanding* adults with
ADD and other learning difficulties

By Sally R. Snowman, Ph.D.

Jones River Press

• Plymouth, Mass. • 1996

Editing and design: Doris M. Johnson, Jones River Press

The information in the book is provided to facilitate the understanding of learning differences. The reader is cautioned against self-diagnosing based on this information. It is highly recommended that a professional diagnosis be sought.

Cataloging-in-Publication Data
Snowman, Sally R. 1951-
Rising to the challenge: A styles approach to understanding adults with ADD and other learning difficulties
90 pages, including foreword, detailed table of contents, appendices; also includes bibliographical references and index.

1. learning styles 2. attention deficit disorder in adults 3. typology (psychology) 4. learning differences/difficulties
I. Title II. Education III. Snowman, Sally R. (author)

ISBN 1-888964-00-6

Printed in the United States of America by Jones River Press *Plymouth, Mass.*

Preface

The information presented in this book is to assist in the understanding of Attention Deficit-Hyperactivity Disorder (ADHD and ADD) and Learning Disabilities (LD) from a "learning styles" perspective. It explores the concept of ADHD/ADD/LD as a unique "style" of acquiring and processing information. Each style brings with it both strengths and stressors. Understanding these can provide invaluable insights into human behavior. The Myers-Briggs Type Indicator (MBTI) is used as an example of a "styles" approach to understand learning differences. Brain-Based Theory is also introduced as a means to gain greater understanding.

Richard Bandler's book *Using Your Brian for a Change*, describes the brain as not having an "off" switch; if not given something to do or to think about it will find its own thing to do. From this description, it appears that all brains can experience ADHD/ADD characteristics to some degree. Many individuals seem to have a natural ability to control their "off" switch; for others it is a life-long struggle.

The strengths and stressors of ADHD/ADD/LD characteristics manifest themselves differently in each individual. Identifying them is the first step in being able to manage them. Such information is not only useful for self-knowledge, but also in understanding others.

The challenge is to actualize our full potential.

Dr. Snowman conducts workshops on such topics as learning styles, total quality management strategies, time management strategies and career exploration.
For workshop information contact:
The Snowman Learning Center
6 Carver Street
Plymouth, MA 02360-3301
508-746-5993

Acknowledgements

The following individuals are recognition for their assistance with this project, either directly or indirectly.

In 1987 Diane Goss and I crossed each others' paths at the Program for Advancement in Learning (PAL) at Curry College, Milton, Mass. I was hired to team-teach with her during a PAL summer intensive session. This progarm is for learning disabled college students attending this four-year liberal arts college. From the onset of us working together, Diane prophesied that some day I was going to make a significant contribution to society. I could not imagine what she saw in me that lead her to this conclusion. Prior to meeting her, I had experienced a major life crisis and was just beginning to emerge out of the rubble. This is included a diagnosis of a learning disability (LD). Nine years later, I am attempting to make a contribution with this book. Diane has been a great supporter in my journey for metacognitive development as I worked through my masters and doctoral programs. Most likely, she has little knowledge of the impact she has had on me. Thank you Diane, for your friendship, foresight and encouragement.

In 1988 I met Leslie Patten (INFP*). She was a new English teacher at Curry College seeking to find out everything she could about learners who processed information differently. She inquired about PAL and how she could best meet the needs of these learners. We instantly bonded. Although Leslie now lives almost 2,000 miles away, we have continued to exchange ideologies as well as many drafts of this book. She has been an invaluable friend and reader.

Shirley Richardson (INFP) has been a significant influence in my life. She just happens to be my oldest sister. As a child I always looked up to her and thought she was the best, and very smart. She moved out into the adult world when I was in 9th grade, and my admiration of her continued. Our relationship translated into the professional realm upon my arrival at Curry, where she was an administrative assistant. I greatly appreciate the time she has taken to read the drafts of this book at a time when she was involved in her doctoral work. But, what sisters are for?

Jay Thomson (ISFJ) is my husband. He has been most tolerant and supportive in this book writing effort within the first year and a half of our

The four letters after the names (ie INFP) indicate the Myers-Briggs descriptors.

marriage. That's love for you! He has learned very quickly the trials and tribulations of living with a learning disabled and ADD wife.

Jay introduced me to his friends Pauline Dulany (ISFP) and Charlie Dulany (ENTJ) who also have been readers for the book. Pauline and I have a lot in common; she is LD and ADD, too. We have had many adventures together! Charlie has been an especially valuable reader because of his Myers-Briggs Type Indicator (ENTJ). It came to me that all the readers were feeling (F) types and it was important to have a "thinker" type on the team. A detail, logically oriented type was needed. Thank you, Charlie, for your "T" perspective.

My parents, Roger and Ginna Snowman, and my other sister, Beverly DeMoratt, have been cheerleaders on the sidelines throughout these efforts. Mum and Papa have always been there for me, not only during traditional child rearing years, but also through the many times when my adult life was in crisis. Thank you for being there for me.

Boston Light, pictured on the book cover, also had a role in the book writing venture. The lighthouse is located on Little Brewster Island situated in the entrance to Boston Harbor, Massachusetts Bay. Portions of the book were written on the island while my husband and I had the privilege of doing lighthouse-keeping duty. We are both members of the U.S. Coast Guard Auxiliary, the volunteer component of the Coast Guard. One of the opportunities available through this organization is relieving one of the "regular" Coast Guard personnel so they can have vacation. Boston Light was the first and is now the last lighthouse to have resident government personnel on its premises. The tranquility of this small island provides much time and inspiration to reflect upon society; where we have been and where we are going. It was a very fitting setting in which to write a book such as this.

Sally R. Snowman, Ph.D.

Table of contents

Quality Education

As we approach the Twenty-First Century, the world is in a ferment to improve the quality of education for its citizens. All agree on the need for quality, but not on what quality is or the best ways to achieve it. The days of educating every one the same way are ending. "Individualizing education" is emerging. Jung's psychological types provide a powerful model for individualizing teaching and learning because it is based on differences in the ways human beings use their minds.

— Mary H. McCaulley
President and Co-Founder
Center for Application of Psychological Type

Chapter 1

Introduction

Walk through any bookstore or browse through mail order catalogs of books, audio and video tapes and you will find an array of information about Attention Deficit-Hyperactivity Disorders (ADHD/ADD) and learning disabilities (LD). With the 21st century quickly approaching, many question *why* there appears to be an epidemic of these labels applied to people of all ages and all walks of life.

There are some who believe that the labels have been fabricated by middle-class society to provide a safe haven for those who are lazy or who through lack of effort are achieving less than their full potential. Those who believe in this fabrication feel that it lowers both society's and the individual's expectations. Consequently, there is often a sense of giving up or learned helplessness by the sufferers of learning difficulties. A frequently made statement is: "If they only tried harder, they would do better."

This book will expose the fallacy of this statement as well as discuss the ADHD/ADD and LD phenomenon in adults.

Why does there appear to be an ADHD/ADD, LD epidemic?

There are three explanations why there appears to be an epidemic of ADHD/ADD and LD. First, although these conditions have existed since the beginning of time, they were not labelled as such until relatively recently. Advancements in scientific research of the brain have specifically identified certain areas and functions of the brain where these difficulties occur.

Secondly, society has become very hi-tech. The information and technological advances require continuous education. Children and adolescents need to be prepared for this. The early diagnoses of learning problems is also a result of such advances. In addition, children with potential learning difficulties are being identified at a very young age.

But what about adults who have struggled through the educational process without the benefit of this high technology? Adults currently in the workforce are recognizing the need for further education to develop new skills to remain employable.

Some adults are now inquiring about their learning difficulties and trying to determine if there has been undiagnosed ADHD/ADD/LD. This appears to be especially true for parents of children who have been diagnosed as ADHD/ADD or LD. They can often recognize patterns that they have in common with their children, and suspect they may have similar problems. There are others who after years of struggling with learning new information or skills are questioning why.

Thirdly, there is current research that substantiates a condition referred to as "classroom trauma." This is caused by learners being traumatized by negative classroom experience which can interfere with their ability for cognitive development. Learning difficulties result. To keep up with hi-tech, adults are entering training and retraining programs as well as vocational and higher education opportunities. Many have been out of formal classrooms for a number of years.

Those who had negative schooling experiences as children may find these feelings recurring as adults. One of the symptoms of such trauma is panic, which results in a physiological imbalance in the brain. Classroom trauma syndrome is further aggravated for those with learning difficulties.

The concept: "Learning across the life-span"

Education has become a lifelong endeavor. Job security demands it. To function properly, a democratic society such as ours depends upon educated citizens.

In order to ensure an educated society, those with learning difficulties need to be identified and strategies developed to assist them so they can be educated contributors in maintaining democracy. Understanding the emotional excess baggage that many adults carry toward formal education due to earlier classroom trauma can assist these learners in overcoming such barriers.

Adults are discovering that the demands of the current workforce frequently require job changes. Until a few years ago, it was common to remain in one job for 40 or more years and then retire. Current trends indicate that it will not be unusual to have five to seven jobs in a 40-year span.

Consequently, the need for continual learning of new skills and acquiring new knowledge through courses, workshops, vocational training, or in-service/on-the-job retraining will be an ongoing

process. Those who have worked in the same kind of job for a number of years may find that to remain in that area will require frequent updates in that field. Others who are seeking to return to the workforce after a few years absence are finding that the skills they had are now outdated.

Adult learners who have been away from formal instructional settings for a while may find the transition back to it difficult. Although a learning difficulty may not have been identified during school-age years, there may be ADHD/ADD and/or LD characteristics emerging with these new learning situations. Or, there may have been undiagnosed learning disabilities or ADHD/ADD that are just now being self-identified and professional help is being sought.

ADHD/ADD and LD population in the U. S.

Diagnoses and labelling of specific learning disabilities began in the 1970s, with ADHD/ADD becoming a prevalent diagnosis in the 1980s. In this book, ADHD/ADD and LD will be combined because, in a global sense, anything that interferes with the learning process can be considered a learning disability.

The percentage of the general population experiencing these disabilities varies anywhere from 7% to 30% depending upon the researchers' frame of reference. Averaging this to 15% of the general population of the United States, we are looking at approximately thirty-eight million (38,000,000) Americans with learning difficulties. These learning difficulties can be truly disabling, possibly interfering with the ability for these citizens to contribute to society to their fullest. What a waste of human potential!!

The challenge

Let's take a look at ways to identify the unique gifts that individuals possess to enable those with learning difficulties to experience their full potential.

Chapter 2

Diagnosing, labelling, getting help

Diagnosing ADHD/ADD/LD

The *Diagnostic and Statistical Manual of Mental Disorders* (DSM-IV) (1994) published by the American Psychiatric Association is the reference "Bible" for determining the existence of Attention Deficit-Hyperactivity Disorder (ADHD/ADD) and Learning Disabilities (LD). The criteria to be met to qualify for the label ADHD/ADD/LD are very specific.

In the DSM-IV, these conditions are considered to be psychologically and medically based disorders of the brain. A recommended resource for learning about the differences between ADHD and ADD can be found in Sari Solden's book, *Women and Attention Deficit Disorder*, pages 24 to 30.

The manner in which ADHD/ADD/LD are usually diagnosed is through a medical evaluation which includes a neuropsychological or psycho-educational assessment. The reason for this is to ensure that there are no other medical or psychological conditions that could be manifesting themselves as a Learning Disability or Attention Deficit-Hyperactivity Disorder.

The labelling for ADHD/ADD/LD occurs only when all other possibilities have been eliminated, for example, seizure disorders, eye problems, brain tumors, hearing problems, psychological problems, and the like. ADHD/ADD diagnosis also requires an extensive life history especially of early childhood years. This is because ADHD/ADD, to be labeled as such, needs to have existed by the age of seven. Once it has been determined no other condition(s) exist which could create these difficulties, a label of ADHD/ADD/LD may then be appropriate.

All diagnoses are not as clear cut as described above. There is a certain percentage of the ADHD/ADD/LD population that may have a combination of both a Learning Disability and an Attention Deficit-Hyperactivity Disorder. This may be a two-step diagnostic process. One may initially be identified, with the second being discovered during the treatment of the first.

There may also be a combination of ADD/ADHD/LD coupled with a psychological condition, such as anxiety or depression. When there is more than one condition involved, it is called a co-morbidity.

Determining which of the conditions may be influencing the other can be a very difficult task. Now, the diagnosis becomes far more complicated.

There is no specific single test which can be utilized to positively identify ADHD/ADD at this time. There are, however, a number of devices that are utilized to evaluate the presence of ADHD/ADD. The evaluator has an array of diagnostic tools choose from. In adults, childhood history plays a significant role in the identification of ADHD/ADD. It is through the process of elimination that the diagnosis is made. Learning disabilities (LD) are more definitively identified because standardized tests are utilized for their identification. ADHD/ADD is more of a qualitative or descriptive diagnosis, where LD is quantitative.

Standardized test scores are the determining factor for labelling of a Specific Learning Disability. There is no process for measuring the presence of ADHD/ADD.

The most difficult diagnosis is identifying ADD without hyperactivity-impulsivity. The outward behaviors that characterize ADHD are not present with ADD. Adults, especially females with ADD, may have a difficult time reconstructing accurate pictures of their childhood experiences, when trying to recall the minute details of their underachievement. They usually remember comments such as being "good" and "sweet," "pleasure to have in the classroom," "average ability," "don't worry about her," "she will do just fine when she is grown."

There is a process which is currently in the research phase that is providing hope for the future in identifying ADHD/ADD. The process is called "SPECT" - Single Photon Emission Computerized Tomography. It utilizes nuclear medicine to study brain activity (metabolism) and blood flow. Dr. Daniel Amen, a psychiatrist in Fairfield, California is breaking ground in this area.

Labelling of ADHD/ADD/LD

Although there is an unfavorable stigma attached to labelling someone ADHD/ADD/LD, we have begun to think of it as a necessary evil. The "label" is the mechanism for receiving "help." The Americans with Disabilities Act (ADA) provides protection from discrimination for citizens with disabilities. These disabilities include ADHD/ADD and/or LD. The law can only assist those who have been diagnosed; without a diagnosis, accommodations can not legally be expected!

Because the labelling is important for acquiring needed accommodations, it is wise to have formal testing to determine the existence of ADHD/ADD/LD.

Testing can be expensive; ranging from $350 to $1,500. Some health insurance providers assist financially with the assessment costs, others do not.

Adults who suspect they have ADHD/ADD/LD and cannot afford the cost of testing are encouraged to pursue self-help avenues. The absence of official labelling does not mean that help is not available. There are a number of ways to learn about ADHD/ADD/LD self-help techniques. Taking responsibility for understanding one's learning difficulties is a major step in the "educational" component.

Joining a support group to network with others experiencing the same types of difficulties, renting videos on the subject, attending lectures and programs offered in the community, and reading books such as this one is a good start. Another avenue is taking a "styles" approach to understanding learning difficulties.

When to be Tested

A question frequently asked is, "When should I seek testing?" Because of the possible expense involved, the best approach may be to find a book or magazine article that describes ADHD/ADD or LD characteristics. If many of the criteria are present, a need for professional help is indicated. Inquire about coverage for such testing with the health insurance provider. Those with coverage, may want to call their family physician and ask for a referral. If this is not possible, look in the yellow pages of the phone book for a psychiatrist, or other professionals who specialize in this area.

The neurological department of major hospitals and medical centers may also be a resource. Whether testing is done or not, if learning difficulties exist, although not professionally diagnosed, help is still available. There are many who specialize in learning issues.

The demand for ADHD/ADD/LD specialists is so great, that some professionals may say they are specialists when they may not have had specific training or extensive experience with this population. Be a good consumer. When making a decision to seek help, make inquiries about years of experience, degrees, licenses, certifications earned, and number of adult ADHD/ADD/LD clients they have successfully serviced.

If learning difficulties are evident, help is available. The following are some of the signs of which to be aware:

- being unable to achieve professional growth because of organizational difficulties,
- being unable to follow written directions,
- having difficulty giving directions,
- having difficulty learning new skills.

Remember – the bottom line is that even without a medical diagnosis, steps can be taken to deal with ADHD/ADD symptoms.

Diagnosis, medication and education of ADHD/ADD

Psychiatrists are physicians (medical doctors) who primarily limit their practice to psychological issues. They can diagnose ADHD/ADD and prescribe medication where appropriate, but they usually do not involve themselves with the educational aspect of the treatment, such as, time management, organizational skills, and the like. Other physicians, such as the family doctor and pediatrician, also diagnose and prescribe. However, they generally leave the ADHD/ADD diagnosis process to others, and primarily write prescriptions.

Psychologists, psychotherapists, counselors, educational therapists, learning specialists, and other health professionals may also be important in identifying ADHD/ADD. These professionals implement the educational and/or psychological components, but they can not prescribe. They usually work as a team with the psychiatrist or other prescribing physician. Therefore, in choosing a testing location, learn who will actually be providing each of these services.

In summary, if ADHD/ADD is diagnosed, know what the process will be. For example: an educational therapist or psychologist may identify the presence of ADHD/ADD, but will not be able to prescribe medication. A physician may diagnose the ADHD/ADD, and provide medication options, but will usually suggest a specialist for the educational component. Either way, it will require a follow-up with another professional. Not being prepared for this may cause an unexpected additional financial hardship.

Diagnosing of learning disabilities (LD)

The testing for learning disabilities is a some what different process than with ADHD/ADD diagnosis. While it may be necessary for the physician to continue to monitor medication doses for the ADHD/ADD, there is usually no need for ongoing supervision in cases of LD.

The physician's role is mainly to rule out any possible medical causes, such as hearing/visual problems, seizures, allergies, and the like, which may be manifesting themselves as learning disabilities. In most cases, treatment is the responsibility of the specialist who not only diagnoses, but also provides the metacognitive processes. This involves learning about the disability and compensating strategies. Medication is usually not used for the treatment of specific learning disabilities.

Getting help

Metacognitive awareness of ADHD/ADD/LD is the process of discovering the "what" and "why" with both the negative and positive aspects. At this point effective coping strategies can be developed. We all have unlimited potential! It just needs to be identified and harnessed.

Although ADHD/ADD/LD are labelled "disabilities" they also have "gifts" to be unlocked. Helping them to find the key is what learning specialists, educational therapists and other specialists are trained to do. Not all have specific training for, or experience working with adults. It is wise to discuss qualifications of the specialists prior to arranging work sessions, to ensure they have the necessary experience to be effective with adults.

It is unfortunate that society has not yet evolved to a point where humaneness is the criteria for providing services. An ideal society would be one where individual differences would be celebrated, and reasonable accommodations be the status quo.

More About Labelling

Individuals have their own unique manner of taking in and processing information. Within this uniqueness, there are patterns of preferences that can be identified, which provide a framework for explaining such differences. Recognizing and categorizing patterns is one of the higher order abilities that only the human brain possesses. The brain's ability to survive is deeply embedded in its ability to identify patterns, draw conclusions, and utilize that information to execute a plan. Categorizing and labelling is an outcome of organizing patterns that have been identified.

Remember, the labels themselves are not harmful. It is utilizing the labels inappropriately that does the harm!

The process of labelling or categorizing provides a way to manage large quantities of information. Labels help to quickly communicate information to others, just as a jar label on the supermarket shelf helps shoppers to identify the product they are looking for.

Labelling of people stirs emotional negativity for many. We need a paradigm shift or a conscious

> **A man ought to read just as inclination leads him; for what he reads as a task will do him little good.**
> • **Boswell's** *Life of Dr. Johnson, Vol. 1,* **Page 266**

effort to change the negative connotations that labels presently hold. Labels are a necessary tool. It is the way our brain is programmed to make sense of all the information that constantly bombards it.

Understanding ADHD/ADD/LD through a learning styles approach is one way to develop effective communications. Everyone processes information in their own unique way. But, there are patterns that can be identified to facilitate communications.

Chapter 3

A "styles" approach to understanding learning difficulties

What are learning styles?

We have, each of us, our own unique preferences – or styles – for acquiring and processing information.

These preferences are a means of explaining and understanding fundamental differences between people. There is no "best" or "preferred" style to have. All styles have their own unique gifts and once identified can be nurtured and positively experienced.

Hundreds of "style inventories" have been developed for self-exploration purposes. They provide a framework for learning about human behavior and preferences.

The one that will be utilized here is the Myers-Briggs Type Indicator, frequently referred to as the MBTI, (both registered trademarks) and published by Consulting Psychologist Press, Inc. This is a very popular and well validated instrument utilized by educators, career counselors, clergy, businesses, and the like. We will be referring to the MBTI as a framework for exploring the concept of learning styles and how it applies to learning difficulties.

What is the Myers-Briggs Type Indicator?

The Myers-Briggs Type Indicator is a self-reporting device that is very useful in helping to identify and understand learning styles.

It was developed by a mother and daughter team, Katharine Briggs and Isabel Briggs Myers, during World War II. This was an expansion upon Dr. Carl Jung's theory of psychological type. Myers and Briggs envisioned world peace being achieved through effective communications rather than warfare.

The MBTI has been successfully utilized for many applications, such as self-development, career development, team building, leadership training, multi-cultural awareness, and the like.

The study and application of the MBTI is referred to as typology. It identifies common patterns in people. Recognizing these patterns is helpful in understanding differences in how information is processed. There are 16 MBTI types, each one possessing its own gifts. We can facilitate our own personal development by identifying and nurturing these unique abilities.

How does ADD Fit into Learning Styles?

Another way to think about ADHD/ADD characteristics is on a continuum. Most people have experienced ADHD/ADD to some degree in their lives. For example, when they:

- take risks,
- interrupt or blurt out answers,
- choose action oriented activities,
- have difficulty with organization and meeting deadlines,
- daydream,
- procrastinate,
- need frequent changes in activities or tasks.

The frequency and intensity of these occurrences determines whether the label ADHD/ADD is appropriate or not.

Considering ADHD/ADD on a continuum provides a framework for utilizing the MBTI to gain self-understanding and learning style preferences.

The frequency and intensity of these occurrences determines whether ADHD/ADD diagnosis is suggested and/or advisable.

Similarities of MBTI and ADHD/ADD descriptors are noteworthy. Some of the descriptions for the 16 MBTI types appear to be similar to ADHD/ADD characteristics. Does this imply that there are certain types that are ADHD/ADD? No! What it *does* suggest is that by looking at a list of ADHD/ADD characteristics, some commonalities emerge. Descriptors, such as, do-think-do, spontaneous, action oriented, does more than one thing at a time, and the like, can be found on an ADHD/ADD check-list as well as on the MBTI.

What needs sorting out is what are considered normal parameters. The following describe the components of the MBTI and a brief summary of each of the 16 types. It is beyond the scope of this book to administer the MBTI, but an understanding of the concept can be determined by reading the descriptions.

The 16 MBTI 'Types'

Myers-Briggs Type Indicator and MBTI are registered trademarks and published by Consulting Psychologist Press, Inc.

ISTJ	ISFJ	INFJ	INTJ
ISTP	ISFP	INFP	INTP
ESTP	ESFP	ENFP	ENTP
ESTJ	ESFJ	ENFJ	ENTJ

E = Extraversion	vs	I = Introversion
S = Sensing	vs	N = iNtuition
T = Thinking	vs	F = Feeling
J = Judging	vs	P = Perceiving

Each of the eight above descriptors have their own definitions that need to be kept in mind when determining a particular type.

These are not dictionary definitions, but have been developed for the specific application of Dr. Jung's theory of typology. The definitions for each are described below.

Extraversion (E) vs Introversion (I)

Extraversion (E) and Introversion (I) indicate from where individuals prefer to get their energy. Extraverts (E) have a preference for acquiring their energy from outside influences. Introverts (I) acquire their energy from within. For example, when at a social setting, Extraverts are energized by the interaction they have with others. They seek to keep the party going and do not want it to end.

Introverts find socializing to be tiresome and look forward to going home. Extraverts have a difficult time winding down after such an event, while Introverts find relief in the solitude of their private space.

Sensing (S) vs Intuition (N)

Sensing (S) and Intuition (N) indicates a preference for taking in and processing information.

Those who gather information through the five senses (see, hear, touch, taste, and smell) fit into the Sensing (S) descriptor.

Intuition (N) describes a preference for gathering information through the "sixth sense" or hunches.

For example, learners with a Sensing (S) preference like having information presented in a practical, detailed, step-by-step manner. They have a tendency to become overwhelmed by the "big picture."

Intuitive (N) learners like to speculate about future possibilities and to be presented the "big picture." They have a tendency to get bogged down if given too much detail.

Thinking (T) vs Feeling (F)

The Thinking (T) and Feeling (F) describe a prefer-

> "I don't think they play at all fairly," Alice began ... "they all quarrel so dreadfully one can't hear oneself speak ... and they don't seem to have any rules in particular; at least if there are, nobody attends to them ... and you've no idea how confusing it is ..."
> *Alice's Adventure in Wonderland*
> **Lewis Carroll**

ence as to how decisions are made.

Thinking (T) types prefer to make decisions based objectively and impersonally using logic, principles and reasoning.

Feeling (F) types make decisions subjectively and sympathetically, taking into account personal values.

Thinkers tend to act for the "common good." They may unintentionally offend others by appearing to be cold-hearted in their decisions. Feelers care about others. They need to be careful not to jeopardize the successful completion of a project in trying to keep everyone involved with it happy.

Judging (J) vs Perceiving (P)

Judging (J) and Perceiving (P) deal with life style preferences.

Judging (J) types prefer a planned and organized life based on schedules and patterns.

Perceiving (P) types enjoy spontaneity, like dealing with problems as they come along, prefer to keep their options open, and tend to postpone unpleasant tasks.

It is important to remember that each of us have all eight of these characteristics within us. We can learn to consciously call on each when required. The following description of the 16 personality types are provided to help in understanding ourselves and others better.

The dynamics of typology

The dynamics of typology goes beyond these individual letter descriptors (I/E, S/N, T/N, J/P). Notice how these eight letters are paired. A preference for one letter in each of the groups provides a four letter combination. This equates to 16 possibilities. These unique interactions are the 16 MBTI personality types.

Brief descriptions of each of the 16 types

ISTJ: organized, factual, good with time management, serious, believes hard work will result in success, detail oriented, likes quiet, work has priority over play, reliable, realistic, decisive.

ISTP: logical, analytical, spontaneous, independent, willing to take risks, quiet, hands-on learner, needs physical activity, knack for maneuvering around rules, adventurous, likes working with hands.

ESTP: likes action, outgoing, spontaneous, easygoing, persuasive, likes experimental learning situations, lots of energy, likes to talk, tends to get lost with abstractions, theories, and details.

ESTJ: organized, decisive, likes routines, pays attention to detail, responsible, matter-of-fact, wants information learned to be immediately applied to real-life, good administrator, structured.

ISFJ: fact oriented, practical, concerned about how others feel, patient, traditional, quiet, procedurally oriented, particular, family oriented, loyal.

ISFP: adaptable, sensitive, spontaneous, personally committed to a cause, likes to create harmony, lives for the here and now, can get caught up in the whirlwind of the immediate situation, not a planner.

ESFP: enthusiastic, playful, sociable, easygoing, outgoing, pleasant, optimistic, generous, conversationalists, may be impulsive, action-oriented, like interruptions from routine.

ESFJ: seeks harmony, conscientious, people-oriented, sociable, responsible, likes routine and predictability, likes the process of decision making, likes tradition, sympathetic, needs to be needed.

INFJ: holistic, visionary, looks at possibilities, concerned with the human condition, sensitive, compassionate, intensive, quietly forceful, idealistic, determined, prefers to work in quiet.

INFP: idealist, looks for patterns and possibilities, sees a global view of reality, empathetic, compassionate, flexible, looks for ways to fulfill human potential.

ENFP: creative, quick with a solution, willingness to help others, good at improvising, enthusiastic, expressive, independent, perceptive, high-spirited, effective at influencing others, nonconformist.

ENFJ: seeks harmony, diplomatic, feels real concern for what others need, sociable, sympathetic, likes to facilitate others to achieve their potential, may prefer verbal communication to writing.

INTJ: independent, innovative, looks for patterns and possibilities, seeks new problems to solve, systems-minded, logical, critical, does not like routine projects and assignments, firm, theoretical.

INTP: theoretical, intellectually curious, solves problems with logic and analysis, theory more important than facts, prefers to work independently without interruptions, sees the "big picture."

ENTP: has many interests, likes intellectual challenges, outspoken, prefers to improvise through a situation rather than plan, project oriented, may have difficulty prioritizing, likes change.

ENTJ: competitive, seeks possibilities, well organized, likes to "take charge", assertive, hard working even at play, natural leaders, solver of organizational problems.

In Summary

Isabel Myers believed that the application of the MBTI would promote the understanding of ourselves as well as others, resulting in improved communications. Effective communications with others require us to know our own point of view, first. We can only begin to understand someone else's view point after we are clear about our own.

Stephen Covey's catchphrase "Seek first to understand, then to be understood" (1989, p. 53), states the MBTI philosophy well.

The MBTI has identified 16 possible types or personality patterns that offer some predictability of human behavior. By applying this to verbal communication, the conversation can be tailored to meet the style of the listener. It is human nature to have differences of opinion and perceptions of the world. Conflicts are going to occur. Realizing and accepting that we have similarities and differences can help us to work through our conflicts.

In the following chapter we will further explore how "typology" can be used to improve the quality of life for those with ADHD/ADD/LD, as well as the rest of society.

[Additional Myers-Briggs Type Indicator (MBTI) information is available in Appendix A.]

Chapter 4

Improving the quality of life and the application of "styles"

Developing effective strategies is a process. ADHD/ADD/LD adults have the challenge to discover and implement effective strategies for coping with various life situations. Such strategies can make the difference between "surviving" or "thriving."

Because ADHD/ADD/LD is uniquely manifested in everyone who experiences it, strategies that work for some may not work for others. There are no guarantees with any one strategy. The key is to remain open-minded throughout the exploration and trial periods. For many, trying something new may not feel comfortable until it becomes familiar.

Therefore, when experimenting with a new strategy, give it a fair chance. Keep working with it until it becomes familiar, then make an educated decision. If the conclusion is that the strategy is not effective or efficient, it may be useful to try to modify it rather than eliminating it.

Analyzing the process is part of the process. If it is working, why? If it is not, why not? Is it worth trying to modify? This will take time and effort also, but it will be worth it. Developing a repertoire of strategies that work well in given situations can become a reference for future tasks.

He that will not set sail until all dangers are over must never put to sea.
• Thomas Fuller

The brain does not function well with:
- **stress**
- **fear**
- **violence**

Establishing effective strategies may not always be an easy task, especially in the beginning. But the more time spent exploring, trying, and fine tuning, the easier and less time consuming it becomes. So, the question that needs to be asked is "what is it worth to you?" It takes a commitment to learn the process and the results are not always immediately measurable.

Therefore, a suggestion is to choose one or two areas in daily life that could benefit from improvement, for example: being on time, keeping important papers organized, getting up on time, grocery shopping, or limiting the time spent talking on the telephone. If choosing a task is difficult make a list of the tasks to be done differently.

Next, prioritize the list by importance, with the most critical on top. For developing effective strategies choose a task that is somewhat important, but not critical. This is important in terms of utilizing the brain to its fullest potential. The brain works best under certain conditions. In learning new strategies, the brain will function best when it is not under a lot of stress.

In fact, there are three conditions in which the brain does not work well: stress, fear, and violence. It responds best to positive experiences. Choosing a task that is important, but not critical, will keep the brain from malfunctioning due to undue pressure while learning something new. Too much emotional pressure to succeed is actually brain antagonistic.

There is a fine line between "challenge" and "stress." When developing strategies to improve the lives of ADHD/ADD/LDers, a challenging environment is required, rather than one of fear or stress. It is true that the brain needs to be emotionally charged to learn, but too much is counterproductive. Stress can occur when there is a sense of fear or failure present, or a feeling that a goal is unobtainable. Again, it is suggested that in the beginning stages of developing effective strategies, choose one or two tasks that are important, but not critical. The brain will respond positively with a successful experience. This will be best served by starting slowly with an obtainable goal.

An Example: Grocery Shopping

The following is an example of an obtainable goal. Kata is an adult who has a very difficult time grocery shopping. Having ADD and paying attention to everything on the overstocked shelves and the huge selections are totally overwhelming to her. Developing coping strategies is a task that Kata considers important but not critical, so it is a good starting point for exploring strategies.

It is suggested that Kata make a list of the items she needs at the store. She shops at one particular store, so she is fairly familiar with the layout. Visualizing the floor plan and where the various items she needs are located, she can either reorganize the list by aisle, or if she is visual, draw a floor plan with the items to be found in each aisle.

The time of day Kata shops is also an important factor for her. It will be best to shop at off-peak hours such as Saturday night. She will want to limit herself to only what is on the list.

Another consideration is the amount of time she allows herself to shop. In past experiences, Kata has left baskets full of groceries behind in the store because she could no longer can stay focused on the task. It is suggested that she place a time limit on shopping before going to the check-out register.

If she finds that 25 minutes is the maximum focus time, it may be helpful to her to ensure that she is at the register within 20 minutes. At this time, whether she has completed collecting the items on her list or not, she will be at the register. This is better than leaving the store without anything. Limiting herself to the 20 minutes may help her to stay focused (or hyper-focused).

If finances are an issue, the combination of having a list and limiting the shopping time may keep Kata from buying impulsively, and prevent her from purchasing things that are not on the list. Shopping at off-peak hours will ensure limited time spent waiting in line at the check-out register. She will have less time to get "nudgy" and this will minimize the urge to walk out of the store before finishing the task.

Kata may also find it helpful to assist with bagging the groceries. The electronic beeping of the bar codes by the register is very distracting to Kata. Bagging groceries will expedite the check-out process as well as give her something other than the beeps to focus on.

Identifying the strategies used in the example

Let's look at the process that Kata went through. She chose one task that she would really like to learn to handle better. It was something low risk in that there would be no significant harm done if she reverted to her old way. She really could not fail! Any piece of the process that was completed could be seen as "success."

The completion of a list would be considered the first accomplishment. Visualizing the location of products on the shelves and the aisles would be the second accomplishment. Going to the store at off-peak hours would be a third. Setting a 20-minute limit to collect the items would be a fourth.

Even if Kata took more time than she allotted, having accomplished the first three steps was worth the effort! She had three successes! Every time she went shopping, she would move toward the established goal.

What Kata may find is that a 20-minute limit is not realistic. But if this is the maximum amount of time she can tolerate, further fine-tuning of the goal can be made. She may benefit by doing two smaller shopping trips over a shorter period of time. Another strategy would be to increase Kata's shopping tolerance over a period of time by gradually increasing shopping time from 20 minutes to 24 minutes to 28, until the required time to fully complete the shopping was accomplished.

Further discussion of the example

The important idea is for Kata to be able to identify the accomplishments she has made. By isolating tasks into small steps, success can be easily seen.

Another important point is that when a goal has not been fully met, Kata needs to identify those parts and re-examine them to determine if the goal is attainable. If not, can an adaptation be made, or would it be best to eliminate the entire strategy? It may be helpful to reality check the strategy results with someone else. This could be a friend, spouse, ADHD/ADD coach, or a professional.

An option for Kata to consider is shopping with a friend who could assist her with pacing out the task. If she starts getting too far astray from the shopping list or spending too much time browsing, the friend can bring this to her attention and suggest that she keep moving.

If a friend is not available, another option may be for Kata to seek an ADHD/ADD coach. The National Coaching Network is an organization that can be contacted to obtain a list of local coaches.

A coach is someone who is contracted to help individuals with establishing goals and "coach" them through the process. The coach will be aware of the uniqueness of ADHD/ADD and will work toward finding strategies that will meet the individuals' needs.

The brain thrives on success. Therefore, Kata's positive experience with shopping brings the confidence to try another task. She will need to continue monitoring her grocery shopping process. It is sometimes very easy to work at something for a short period of time and then slowly return to old habits.

It will be best if Kata consciously reminds herself of the shopping process until it becomes second nature to her. The ADHD/ADD/LD brain needs repeated reinforcement for the pattern to be permanently stored. How long the process takes will depend upon the individuals and the tasks being learned. Do not rush it! It will take time to ensure that the process is permanently learned by the brain. This will take perseverance.

The one attribute that is characteristic of all those who have been successful is "perseverance." This, too, can be learned.

The importance of perseverance

Typology can be helpful in understanding why some people seem to be able to persevere while others have great difficulty with it. It is something that everyone can develop if they want to.

This brings us back to the question: "How much is it worth to you?" Having a passion for something helps develop perseverance. When something is important enough, sacrifices can be made.

In this example, Kata has to give up her random ways. She needs to take the time to make her list, to visualize where the items are in the store, change her usual schedule to shop, and to hyper-focus on what she is doing in the store.

The first few times Kata does this will seem foreign to her. It may feel really uncomfortable. She will need to decide for herself whether the time and effort she is putting into this is going to be worth it in the long run. She may decide after a six weeks' trial that her helter-skelter way is her "style" and works better for her.

If it is her lifestyle she is working toward improving, it may be in her best interest to try this shopping strategy a while longer. Changing life patterns takes time, and commitment. If Kata does not buy into the process, it will not work for her.

This is where understanding the concept of a self-

Consider the postage stamp: its usefulness consists in the ability to stick to one thing till it gets there.
• Josh Billings

fulfilling prophecy can be important. Believing that all the perseverance and strategy development will not help will be a self-fulfilling prophecy: it will not help. Believe that there is a better life out there for the ADHD/ADD/LD adult and make a commitment to finding it, and it will be so.

Application of Myers-Briggs Type Indicator (MBTI)

There are certain MBTI types that appear to have ADHD/ADD/LD characteristics. Taking a styles approach provides: (1) the ability for self-understanding, and (2) the ability to understand and communicate with others. Research indicates that our minds function best when preferred mental processes are utilized.

Metacognition is the individuals' knowledge of how their brain acquires information. The MBTI provides a tool for metacognitive exploration. It also provides a means for "normalizing" ADHD/ADD/LD'ness since many MBTI types have similar descriptors.

Diagnosing ADHD/ADD can be difficult. The question is, again, do those MBTI types with ADHD/ADD descriptors have ADHD/ADD? This question can be best answered through the following examples.

An example is the **Sensing-Perceiving (SP)** types. Statistically, SPs have the highest high school drop-out rate. Why is this? Understanding the brain's preference for taking in and processing information provides us with some insight.

The SPs prefer to have hands-on, experiential learning and therefore learn best when able to directly experience the information they are expected to know.

SPs can easily get bogged down with schedules, plans, and deadlines. Traditional classroom settings are not their style; the routine schedule of classroom work mainly consists of listening to lectures, taking

If A equals success, the the formula is A = X + Y + Z.
X is work.
Y is play.
Z is keep your mouth shut.
• Albert Einstein

notes, and completing structured assignments. Memorization of facts is very difficult for SPs unless they are able to place the data into time references that make sense to them.

SPs perform best when they have choices and they know why and/or how the information is going to be useful to them in the future.

The similarities between ADHD/ADD and SP characteristics appear to be comparable. But as stated earlier, this does not mean they are all ADHD/ADD. Look at this as a continuum or a matter of degree. Are the SPs' characteristics severe enough to be interfering with the ability to self-actualize?

Examples of similar descriptors are: seeks excitement, a risk-taker, procrastinates, difficulty with meeting deadlines, difficulty with authoritarian figures, difficulty with organization, and difficulty with following through.

These can appear to be negative aspects of SP types. SP adults excel in environments where they have options, can work at their own pace, choose the order of priority, and feel their contributions are appreciated. Tasks that are personally of high interest and importance to them fit the following SP descriptors: high energy, the ability to meet deadlines, respects authoritarian figures, follows through, and organized.

The bottom line is that ADHD/ADD characteristics of SPs are minimal when they are in their element.

This brings us to another point. ADHD/ADD seems to be most evident when adults are in environments that are not conducive to their style. Place them in a more user-friendly environment, and their ADHD/ADD appears to go away. But does it, really? By taking a styles approach to understanding differences, we can begin to understand that the environment is an important element in diminishing or increasing the degree of ADHD/ADD manifestations.

There are other MBTI types that also have ADHD/ADD characteristics. For example the intuitive-feeling-perceiving types (NFPs) are concerned with the human condition. They are not good with details, far preferring to look at the big picture.

Introverted NFPs can appear to be spacy. "Paying attention" to a lecture with statistical facts may be overwhelming because their brains have difficulty attaching the details to form the big picture. For them, such settings may feel brain antagonistic. Specific examples of how these facts impact upon humans is what NFPs want to know about. They are good at problem solving, looking at possibilities that are not readily (concretely) apparent.

Extraverted NFPs may be apt to blurt out their thoughts without thinking about how their comment will be received by the educator/presenter. This is often interpreted as unacceptable behavior. However, thinking out loud or talking it out helps the ENFPs to process their ideas.

Does this make all NFPs ADHD/ADD? No! The frequency and intensity of these will be determining factors in seeking professional help.

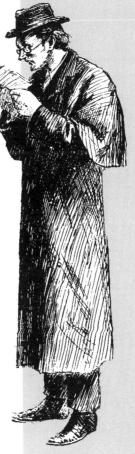

A styles approach to understanding differences

How necessary is an ADHD/ADD label in order for individuals or society to value them as citizens?

A styles approach helps us to understand that individuals have their own style or preference for taking in and processing information. Society needs to develop tolerance and begin to appreciate the unique gifts that we all possess. There are ways to identify what those gifts are and to further develop them.

ADHD/ADD appears to carry with it negative connotations. By looking at it as a style, the gifts are much more obvious. Viewing an ADHD/ADD as being the extreme of the continuum, "off the Richter scale," gives us a framework to work with the positive attributes that all individuals possess. Identifying each strength and building on those strengths will bring successes that can be further developed.

Diagnosing ADHD/ADD is most critical for

those who do not perceive themselves as performing to their full potential, and/or feel that they have a lot more to offer; but are clueless as to what it is, or how to access it.

It is important to understand that some individuals with ADHD/ADD may require medications to help them focus; others may only need the educational component.

Those who are able to have an "ah ha" experience, suddenly learning about their gifts and how to access them, describe this as a powerful encounter. Some may need medications to do this, others may not.

So if ADHD/ADD is a consideration, think about it from a styles approach. Life may become more manageable through self-help. It may not be necessary to go through an extensive, expensive ADHD/ADD diagnosis to learn how to self-actualize.

There are many methods to choose from. These options include: independent self-help; working with coaches, support groups, and/or professionals. The goal is to improve the quality of life.

"Who in the world am I? Ah, *that's* the great puzzle!"
Alice's Adventure in Wonderland
• Lewis Carroll

Chapter 5

Brain-based learning theory

Brain-based learning theory is a relatively new concept in this country. It provides a means for maximizing the brain's full potential.

The brain is a three-pound mass that loves to learn. It is very inquisitive. It has lots of energy that needs to be harnessed and specifically directed to maximize its full potential. It has a habit of doing its own thing. All brains have this tendency, not just those of ADHD/ADD/LDers.

Eric Jensen (1995) describes the brain as a "jungle with no one in control." Through conscious effort, we have the ability to learn how to control it. Some people appear to have an easier time than others taming their brains. Brain-based learning theory provides a means for taking control.

Recognizing there is so much more to learn,

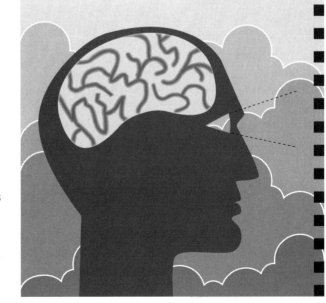

reseraches are continuing the quest to understand the brain and how it works. However, an important and established fact is, that the more the brain is used, the better it functions. It likes to problem solve. The brain can be harnessed and there are a lot of theories about how to do this. Brain-based theory looks at positive features, such as recognizing patterns, allowing it to work effectively and efficiently. The more patterns it can identify, the more inroads it can make. The challenge is in mastering our own unique brain to our advantage.

Learning styles and brain-based theory

A styles approach to understanding learning differences is compatible with brain-based theory. The brain performs at its best when information is presented in the style the brain prefers. This is how it can make the quickest connections. Therefore, by knowing about preferred learning styles, learners can take charge of their learning environment.

This can be done in a number of ways. It would be nice if the people we interact with were all familiar with styles and automatically communicated in our preferred mode. Unfortunately, this is not realistic. However, we can help ourselves. The following are four possible suggestions:

1. Know what our preferences are. For example, in MBTI terms, Intuitive/Perceiving (NP) types have a tendency to prefer information to be given "whole-to-parts," wanting to see the big picture. Details are not their strong point.

2. Be able to accept ourselves as we are.

3. Be able to explain to others our preference for receiving information. For example, Sensing/Judging (SJ) types have a tendency to need details presented in a sequential manner, "parts-to-whole," with few digressions. When having a

conversation with someone who has gone on a tangent, having digressed from the topic, they can be brought back on track by (a) restating the information that was received and (b) asking a specific question.

4. When others are not communicating to us in our preferred mode, we need to translate it into our preferred manner. For example, for those who are best at processing visual information, receiving verbal directions may be difficult. The strategy is to translate the information received into a visualization.

Ask if the information has been written down. If so, obtain a copy of it. If not, ask for it to be written down, or allow for the conversation to be audio taped. Those with a strong visual memory, visualizing the information in the "third eye" may also be effective.

The wind and the waves are always on the side of the ablest navigators.
• Edward Gibbon

Importance of self-advocacy skills

Self-advocacy is a skill in itself. It may be difficult, at first, for many to do this. The ability to communicate effectively is a very valuable life skill. It may be beneficial to work with a professional or a coach to help learn about such strategies. The time and effort taken to develop such skills will be well worth it.

Effective communication requires that the people communicating be on the same wave length. Knowing something about styles can improve the likelihood of this occurring.

Communication requires the interaction of both speakers and listeners. The more they have in common (alike types), the more likely they will be on the same wave length. The less they have in common (opposite types), the more effort it may take.

For example: Alike types such as ISTJs/ISTJs usually connect quickly with each other; ISTJs/

ENFPs (complete opposite types) may need to be aware of and be tolerant of their differing points of view, and work toward being on the same wave length.

According to brain-based theory, a lot more goes on between speaker and listeners than just the words that are being used. The brain is processing a multitude of information, both consciously and subconsciously with the brain taking in the entire environment: noting peripheral sights, sounds and aromas.

The ADHD/ADDers may be distracted by any of these, while others may be unaware of them. Brain-based theory suggests that we provide brain compatible experiences. For example, considering visual, auditory, or kinestheic preferences, draw a map for those with a visual preference, rather than giving them verbal directions. By knowing our own styles, we can take control of what we want to do with our lives.

NeuroLinguistic Programming (NLP)

NeuroLinguistic Programming (NLP) is another piece of brain-based theory. It was developed in the 1970s by Richard Bandler to (1) help people understand themselves, and (2) develop effective communication skills.

NLP is about attitude (or a state of mind) as well as strategies and techniques to develop skills. To communicate well with others we must first understand ourselves. NLP is a process for improving the quality of life, for those who are ready to meet the challenge.

NLP provides a framework for us to look at what we do and to find alternative solutions. The desire to change must come from within each individual. Most of our behaviors have been learned. If we are not pleased with our performance, we can unlearn unwanted behaviors and replace them with desirable ones.

Richard Bandler describes the brain as not having an "off" switch. If it is not given something to do or to think about, it will find its own thing to do. This description seems to imply that all brains are naturally ADHD/ADD; it is just a matter of how this tendency

Experience shows that success is due less to ability than to zeal. The winner is he who gives himself to his work–body and soul.
• **Charles Buxton**

manifests itself and how individuals harness it. Some people seem to have a natural ability to control their "off" switch; for others, it is a life-long struggle.

NLP provides a means of taking control and consciously manipulating the brain to be more functional and efficient. It enables us to better control ADHD/ADD tendencies.

An Example of NLP in Action

Kata's situation described in Chapter 4 is an example of how NLP can be used to change behavior. Grocery shopping is totally overwhelming for Kata. She wants to become more efficient at it. She does not want to continue the way she currently shops. NLP provides the framework to change behavior to something more tolerable.

One of the strategies that Kata may try is to begin by limiting the amount of time she allows herself to shop, for example 20 minutes. She can gradually increase shopping time to 24 minutes, then to 28 minutes until the needed time to complete the shopping can be tolerated. By setting up this structure, and with perseverance and practice, she will be able to do it.

It is the practicing that helps the brain learn the new pattern. NLP is the development of programs that communicate the desired behaviors to the brain.

Therefore, to ensure the pathways of the brain are properly routed requires a fair amount of time, commitment and effort. NLP is the developing of such patterns. This process may be facilitated by the assistance of a coach or professional.

Visual, auditory, and kinesthetic/tactile (VAKT) preferences

Another piece to NeuroLinguistic Programming (NLP) is exploring preferences for acquiring information by visual (V), auditory (A), or kinesthetic/tactile (K/T) experiences.

• Visual (V) learners learn best by seeing, reading, or being shown information that is being presented.

• Auditory (A) learners prefer listening, talking to others, and having information explained to them.

• Kinesthetic/tactile (K/T) learners prefer being able to physically touch things and physically move around. Tactile (T) experiences refers to using the hands, such as molding clay and manipulating small objects (beans, paper clips, popcorn). Kinesthetic (K) experiences refer to using the whole body in large movements, such as with roller blading, walking, and pantomimes. Sometimes tactile is included with kinesthetic since they both require movement, either large or small motor coordination.

Most individuals can function adequately as learners with any of the three styles (V, A, or K/T). But, approximately 20% of the learners have much difficulty processing information that is not presented in their preferred style. Michael Grinder (1991) describes these learners as needing to have information "translated" into their preferred style for it to be properly stored in the brain.

Identifying our preferred sensory channel (visual, auditory, or kinesthetic/tactile) will provide further insights into understanding our learning style.

This is especially true for those who are primarily kinesthetic/tactile (K/T) learners. The auditory (A) learners have the greatest advantage in traditional classroom settings because it requires mostly listening skills. The kinesthetic (K) learners are at the greatest disadvantage because they need movement to process information effectively. Fidgeting, rocking the chair, or walking around the room are not considered acceptable behaviors. Visual (V) learners are not always accommodated for, either.

This leaves the visual and kinesthetic/tactile learners to accommodate themselves. They can benefit from developing effective learning strategies to translate auditory information into their preferred style.

An example: Camden is taking an English Composition course at the local community college. His preferred learning style is kinesthetic/tactile. Organizing his thoughts is difficult for him. The instructor requires outlines of proposed papers before the composition is written.

Because this is not an easy task for him, Camden usually waits until the last possible moment to do his handwritten assignments. He does his best thinking when he is outdoors doing yard work, walking, or playing ball. Rather than sitting down to compose the paper, he may do better doing something physical while thinking about what he wants to write. The ideas can be manipulated in his head.

When ideas are well formulated in his head, he is then ready to write them down. A computer can be very helpful, because he can see words clearly on the screen.

Using a keyboard is very tactile! He can dump all the ideas, however random they may be, onto the screen. Once the thoughts are there, he can then use the "cut and paste" word processing features to sequence the thoughts. He does not have to censor what he dumps onto the screen; he just lets it flow.

To produce an outline for his instructor, Camden makes a copy of his "dumping document" to edit. He deletes all but the major points he wants to make, edits it to look like an outline, and submits it.

The original document is still available for editing into the final paper. The instructor never

> **"I think I should understand that better,"** Alice said very politely, **"if I had it written down, but I can't quite follow it as you say it."**
>
> *Alice's Adventure in Wonderland*
> **• Lewis Carroll**

needs to know that the outline was done out of sequence! Some learners need to get all their thoughts out first, before they can organize them into a logical sequence for the final paper.

Effective use of NeuroLinguistic Programming (NLP) requires us to understand and use VAKT preferences to assist us in affecting positive change. Suggested resources listed in the back of this book to further explore VAKT concepts include Jensen's *Brain-based Learning and Teaching* (1995) and Bandler's *Using Your Brain for a Change* (1985).

Right Brain/Left Brain/Whole Brain Theory: more of NLP

There have been many books written about "whole brain" thinking. An over-simplification, but effective description, of our brain is that it has two halves or hemispheres connected by a mass of fibers referred to as the Corpus Callosum. This fibrous mass provides the means for the right and the left sides of the brain to communicate with each other.

Research has found that each side of the brain prefers to process certain types of information. Understanding this preference can help explain why our brains seem to get "stuck" at times.

The right side of the brain prefers to process information by taking in the "big picture." It does not particularly like details, but rather likes to get the "gist" of the situation. It likes to identify patterns.

The left side of the brain prefers to focus on the details. It likes to receive information in a sequential, step-by-step format, and can easily identify numbers and letters.

Whole-brain thinking advocates knowing when to tap into the left side of the brain and when to access the right.

When reading, the left brain identifies the letters and words; the right provides the context for understanding.

The right side of the brain is drawn to colors, graphics, pictures and taking in the whole picture; the left side focuses on the details. In conversations, the left side of the brain focuses on the words that are being said, the right side picks up on the intonations of the voice and reads body language.

Knowing the preferences of each side of the brain can help us consciously switch to the side that is appropriate for a particular situation.

For example, before balancing the checkbook after proofreading a paper — both left-brain, detailed activities — take a walk. This right-brained activity provides the brain with a well needed break to avoid overload.

Simplification of right- and left-brain references

LEFT	RIGHT
• processes logic	• processes visual information
• analyses	
• words	• images
• details	• "big picture"
• "parts-to-whole"	• "whole-to-parts"
• sequence	• random
• organizes	• abstractions
• facts	• theoretical
• likes structure	• intuitive
• serious	• playful
• listening	• visualization
• auditory	• feelings and emotions
• reality	• fantasy

Brain Gym: Another brain-based method

Brain Gym is a self-help program developed by Paul E. Dennison in the 1970s. Kinesthetics are used in the educational process. It is the interdependence of physical development, language acquisition, and academic achievement. Brain Gym is a trademark of Educational Kinesiology Foundation of Ventura, CA. Dennison defines "Edu-Kinesthetic as the study and application of specific movements which activate the brain for optimal storage and retrieval of information." It is learning through natural movement experiences.

Brain Gym helps open communication between the left and right side of the brain. The purpose of these exercises is to cross the midline of the body. The left side of the brain controls the right side of the body; and the right side of the brain controls the left side of the body.

When only one side of the brain is accessed, there is body imbalance. The mind and body can not be separated; one affects the other. Brain-based theory strives to create a healthy mind-body integration. The flow of communication between the two halves of the brain through the Corpus Callosum, can be assisted by Brain Gym.

The key to Brain Gym is unlocking learning potential, by identifying the specific exercises that work best for us. This is a whole-brain learning experience through simple body movements.

Individuals of all ages experiencing academic difficulties, such as dyslexia, distractibility, and hyper-activity find Brain Gym exercises helpful. These learners have a tendency to have difficulty with crossing over the midline. Focusing and centering are important brain functions that require this midline crossing.

Brain Gym exercises are a simple means of achieving mind-body balance. This is a whole brain approach that is not limited to helping those with learning difficulties, but can also be applied to work environments to increase productivity and improve communications. What works well for those with LD works well for all!

Brain Gym is a strategy or technique for repatterning the brain. Positive changes have occurred when doing specific exercises prior to beginning an activity that is not comfortable such as needing to pay attention to detail, following through, organizing paperwork, staying on schedule, carrying out instructions, accessing memory, handling criticism, staying calm, planning long-range strategies. There are specific exercises for each required task.

The Brain Gym exercise names may sound strange, but they are effective. For example: Balance Buttons, Gravity Glider, The Energy Yawn, Lazy 8s, The Owl, and Double Doodle. These movements are designed to stimulate, release, or relax.

The movements of these Brain Gym exercises help to stimulate all parts of the brain and help it to integrate, resulting in better verbal communications, problem solving, organizing, and thinking.

The Resource section of this book provides information on how to access Brain Gym publications.

Multiple intelligences

This chapter would not be complete without mentioning Howard Gardner's theory of the Multiple Intelligences. He believes that too much emphasis has been placed on the two kinds of intelligences that are measured by intelligence tests: Logical-Mathematical and Linguistic (verbal).

Gardner has identified five additional intelligences: spatial, musical, bodily-kinesthetic, Interpersonal, and Intrapersonal. All seven are equally valuable, and deserve to be nurtured and appreciated.

Individuals possess all of these intelligences to some degree, but there are usually one or two that are especially strong. The challenge is to identify the strengths and effectively apply them to accomplish life goals.

There are no "standardized tests" to measure the level of these seven intelligences in individuals. Individuals need to determine for themselves which intelligences they believe are their strengths, and develop active learning strategies based upon those descriptions.

There are many professionals who are familiar with Gardner's theory and will be able to help those who wish to learn more about them. Below is a very brief overview of each of the seven intelligences.

Linguistic Intelligence is having a natural ability with words, written, verbal or both. Verbal ability may be demonstrated through debating, entertaining, or teaching. Ability to write essays, stories, poetry, or journalism are other examples of Linguistic Intelligence.

Logical-Mathematical Intelligence is an ability for working with numbers and thinking logically. Many scientists, accountants, and computer programmers rate themselves high in this intelligence. They have the ability to think in terms of cause-and-effect and create hypotheses.

Spatial Intelligence is having a natural ability for thinking in terms of pictures and images. Many architects, photographers, artists, and mechanical engineers identify Spatial Intelligence as their gift.

Musical Intelligence is possessing the ability to perceive and appreciate music. Many who rate themselves high in the intelligence can play a musical instrument, write music, or sing.

Bodily-Kinesthetic Intelligence is the ability to have good control of body movements and/or handle objects with skill. These people have a need to move and use "gut" feelings in making decisions. A wide range of occupations and activities fall into this category, such as: carpenters, surgeons, mechanics, and outdoor sport enthusiasts (ie hikers, swimmers).

Interpersonal Intelligence is the ability to understand other people. These people may find themselves attracted to professions that require interacting with others, such as social directors, administrators, and teachers.

Intrapersonal Intelligence is understanding our innerselves; having the ability for self-reflection. Many with this intelligence are drawn to "helping" professions, such as counselors and religious leaders. They seek to help others understand themselves.

Three recommended books for further exploration into the theory of multiple intelligences are: *7 Kinds of Smart* by Thomas Armstrong, (1993) *Frames of Mind: The Theory of Multiple Intelligences* by Howard Gardner, (1983) and *Seven Ways of Knowing* by David Lazear (1991).

We all have these multiple intellengences. However, we usually have an inborn perference for one or two of these; they need to be nutured. Except for the few individuals who have been able to gain fame, society has not always valued many of these intelligences, such as musical and bodily-kinethestic. Self-esteem tends to dwindle without encouragement and support. We need to feel good about the talents we possess and not consider one intelligence more valuable than another.

Emotional Intelligence (EQ)

Emotional Intelligence is the ability to manage our emotions effectively for the various situations in which we find ourselves. Feeling too much may cause us to over-react to a situation or misinterpret what actually happened. Too little feeling may cause us to be "insensitive" or "cold hearted."

Emotions are a part of human behavior that can bring both pleasure and misery. The ultimate goal is to be able to harness the positive energy that emotions provide us and to minimize the negative aspects. Daniel Goleman's book *Emotional Intelligence* (1995) discusses these concepts extensively.

EQ can be considered a part of the multiple intelligence theory. Although Howard Gardner has not specifically identified EQ as one of the seven intelligences, it is included in the Interpersonal and Intrapersonal Intelligences. Descriptions such as "self-reflection" and "understanding others" implies "social savvy" or EQ.

Goleman describes our brain as having two parts: the "thinking" part and the "feeling" part. EQ refers to how these two interact with each other. The emotional or feeling brain has existed since the beginning of human evolution. The thinking or rational brain has evolved over millions of years. The emotional brain was necessary for survival. Its ability to read the environment instantly to identify and respond to dangers was a necessity: "kill or be killed." Instant reflexes were very handy back then. Today's society requires different survival skills. Recognizing the need to be held accountable for our actions calls for a more thoughtful, reflective way of thinking.

Although we now have a thinking or rational brain, the feeling or emotional brain is still very much with us. Both offer advantages as well as disadvantages in various situations. The task is to seek balance between the two.

Emotions add a quality to our lives. It allows us to appreciate a beautiful sunrise, and feel good about working on a difficult task.

Current research indicates that those who are able to harness their emotional energy, and to direct it positively, have happier, more fulfilling lives than those whose emotions are less directed. The good news is that we can learn to harness our emotions; we can gain control over how we respond to our emotions. To optimize our full potential, we need to seek balance between the rational and emotional portions of the brain.

EQ seems to be a reoccurring theme through much of the literature about ADHD/ADD/LD, although not being specifically called EQ. For example: Thom

Hartmann (1993) discusses ADD in terms of the "hunter" and the "farmer" in his book *Attention Deficit Disorder: A Different Perception;* the MBTI's "Sensing" and "Feeling" descriptions; and right/left brain descriptions. What this means is that there is a wealth of information out there to help us understand our own unique style of perceiving the world. They all support the premise that it is possible to take control of our minds and our lives.

In Summary

The only way for us to change is to be responsible for changing ourselves. The first step is to understand how we, as individuals, acquire (take in) and process information. Brain-based theory has successfully been placed into practice to help learners of all ages to maximize their full potential. Adults with ADHD/ADD/LD have found learning styles, Brain Gym activities, multiple intelligence theory, VAKT, and NLP reprogramming of the brain to be highly effective in affecting change. They all provide concrete ways to begin taking responsibility for ourselves and to seek higher levels of accomplishment. There is a wealth of human resources available to help us in this quest, such as health professionals, educational specialists, and coaches. A number of organizations are provided in the Resource section of this book.

I have sometimes dreamt, at least, that when the Day of Judgment dawns and the great conquerors and lawyers and statesmen come to receive their rewards – their crowns, their laurels, their names carved indelibly upon imperishable marble – the Almighty will turn to Peter and will say, not without a certain envy when he sees us coming with our books under our arms, "Look, these need no reward. We have nothing to give them here. They have loved reading."

"How Should One Read a Book?", *The Second Common Reader*
• Virginia Woolf

Chapter 6

Rising to the challenge: pulling it all together

The challenge is to facilitate the evolution of a humane society through a kinder, gentler, more mindful understanding of differences. The concepts presented in this book are specifically directed toward helping ADHD/ADD/LDers understand themselves and to provide a foundation to begin self-exploration.

Stephen Covey, in his book *The Seven Habits of Highly Effective People* (1989), emphasizes that psychological survival depends upon each and every one of us feeling that we are understood, affirmed, validated, and appreciated. He stresses the importance to "seek first to understand, then to be understood."

Until we understand and accept ourselves, our path toward self-actualization may tend to be haphazard at best, and may be filled with disappointment and despair.

There is a lot of confusion and contradictory information about learning disabilities and especially attention deficit-hyperactivity disorder. The thought of placing all those with ADHD/ADD/LD in one pot to recommend a one-fix-for-all is not possible.

The manifestation of ADHD/ADD/LD is truly unique for the individuals who experience it. No two ADHD/ADD/LDers are alike. Certain characteristics and patterns may appear the same, but the actual manifestation creates very unique circumstances. What works for some may not work for others.

In Chapter 3, common personality patterns were identified, and it was acknowledged that individual uniquenesses exist within these 16 types. The same is true with ADHD/ADD/LDers. There are some characterstics that are shared, while others are truly unique.

When we are not performing in areas of our expertise, style, or comfort level, ADHD/ADD/LDness has a tendency to permeate our actions and thoughts be it with parenting, relating or managing. A great analogy described by Richard Lavoie is that of a water bed; when one person moves everyone feels the ripples.

Formal ADHD/ADD/LD assessements administered by "professionals" can be helpful in providing pieces to the puzzle; but the uniqueness that ADHD/ADD/LDers experience can best be probed through self-exploration. Sharing the findings of these

self-exploration efforts with a professional will facilitate a team approach toward solving the puzzle.

"Seek first to understand . . . "

Typology provides us a means to better understand ourselves and others. Knowing ourselves is the first step toward effective communication with others. Therefore, "know thyself." The second task is to identify the listeners' preferred style of acquiring information and appeal to that style. Expecting to identify styles of others before we understand ourselves is not sound practice. Only after we understand ourselves and the listerner can we expect to communicate effectively.

The ability to identify what we need, why we need it, and express these needs in terms others can understand is also very important. Failing to do this may lead them to believe they understand us when they do not.

Lack of effective communication leads to misunderstandings, disappointment, and to the demise of self-esteem, perpetuating the downward spiral that so many ADHD/ADD/LDers are all too familiar with.

The Quest

Each one of us has to identify, for ourselves, how our ADHD/ADD/LDness is manifesting itself and what we can do to advocate for ourselves. Education and self-understanding are necessary beginnings in the life-long endeavor toward self-actualization.

Educational sources can include: reading available literature (books, magazines, journals, pamphlets), watching specials or videos on TV, attending community lectures and support groups, talking and sharing experiences with others, consulting with coaches, health and/or educational professionals.

There are many options available to be explored. Do not settle for something that does not feel comfortable. Pursue other alternatives. If in doubt about something heard or read, check it out with another source. Take what you want and leave the rest. The challenge is for ADHD/ADD/LDers to define their own characteristics and identify strategies and techniques that will work for them.

Consider this a quest rather than a burden. Let's accept the challenge to take control of our own lives! This will be an empowering experience, allowing us to deal with our ADHD/ADD/LDness rather than blaming ourselves or others because of it.

Books are keys to wisdom's treasure;
Books are gates to lands of pleasure;
Books are paths that upward lead;
Books are friends. Come, let us read.
Inscription in Children's Reading
Room, Hopkington, Mass.,
written by Emilie Poulsson

References

Amen, D. (1995). <u>Images into the mind: A radical new look at understanding and changing behavior.</u> Fairfield, CA: Mind Works Press.

American Psychiatric Association. (1994). <u>Diagnostic and statistical manual of mental disorders (4th ed.) [DSM-IV]</u>. Washington, D.C.

Armstrong, T. (1993). <u>7 kinds of smart: Identifying and developing your many intelligences.</u> New York, NY: Penguin Books USA, Inc.

Bandler, R. <u>Using your brain for a change</u>. Moab, Utah: Real People Press.

Covey, S. (1989). <u>The seven habits of highly effective people: Restoring the character ethic.</u> New York, NY: Simon & Schuster, Inc.'

Dennison, P.E., & Dennison, G.E. (1989). <u>Brain gym: Teacher's edition revised</u>. Ventura, CA: EduKinesthetics, Inc.

Gardner, H. (1983). <u>Frames of mind: The theory of multiple intelligences.</u> New York, NY: Basic Books, Inc.

Goleman, D. (1995). <u>Emotional intelligence</u>. New York: Bantan Books.

Grinder, M. (1991). <u>Righting the educational conveyor belt (2nd ed.)</u>. Portland, OR: Metamorphous Press.

Hartmann, T. (1993). <u>Attention deficit disorder: A different perception.</u> Novator, CA: Underwood-Miller.

Jensen, E. (1995). <u>Brain-based learning & teaching</u>. Del Mar, CA: Turning Point Publishing.

Keirsey, D., Bates, M. (1984). <u>Please understand me: Character and temperament types</u>. Del Mar, CA: Prometheus Nemesis Book Company.

Lavoie, R.D. (1994). <u>Video: Learning disabilities and social skills: Last one picked .... first one picked on.</u> Washington, D.C.: WETA

Lazear, D. (1991). <u>Seven ways of knowing: Understanding multiple intelligences (2nd ed.)</u>. Palatine, IL: Skylight Publishing, Inc.

Myers, I.B., & McCaulley, M.H. (1985). <u>Manual: A guide to the development and use of the Myers-Briggs Type Indicator</u>. Palo Alto, CA: Consulting Psychologists Press, Inc.

Saunders, F.W. (1991). <u>Katherine and Isabel: Mother's light, daughter's journey</u>. Palo Alto, CA: Consulting Psychologists Press, Inc.

Solden, S. (1995). <u>Women with attention deficit disorder: Embracing disorganization in the workplace</u>. Grass Valley, CA: Underwood Books.

Resources

Recommended ADD/ADHD Books

Amen, D.G. (1995). <u>Images into the mind: A radical new look at understanding and changing behavior</u>. Mind Works Press, 2220 Boynton Avenue, Suite C, Fairfield, CA 94533. (707)-429-7181

American Psychiatric Association. (1994). <u>Diagnostic and statistical Manual of Mental Disorders</u>. American Psychiatric Association, 1400 K Street, N.W., Washington, DC 20005.

Copland, E.D. & Copps, S.C. (1995). <u>Medications for attention disorders (ADHD/ADD) and related medical problems: A comprehensive handbook</u>. Plantation, FL: Specialty Press, Inc.

Copps, S.C. (1992). <u>The attending physician: Attention deficit disorders: A guide for pediatricians and family physicians</u>. Atlanta, GA: SPI Press.

Gordon, M., & McClure, (1996). <u>The down & dirty guide to adult ADD</u>. DeWitt, NY: GSI Publications. Inc.

Hallowell, E.M., & Ratey, J.J. (1994). <u>Driven to distraction</u>. New York, NY: Pantheon Books.

Hallowell, E.M., & Ratey, J.J. (1994). <u>Answers to distraction</u>. New York, NY: Pantheon Books.

Hartmann, T. (1993). <u>Attention deficit disorder: A different perception</u>. Novato, CA: Underwood-Miller.

Hartmann, T. (1994). <u>Focus your energy: Hunting for success in business with attention deficit disorder</u>. New York, NY: Simon & Schuster.

Hunsucker, G. (1998). <u>Attention deficit disorder</u>. Fort Worth, Texas: Forest Publishing.

Ingersoll, B.D., & Goldstein, S. (1993). <u>Attention deficit disorders and learning disabilities: Realities, myths and controversial treatments</u>. New York, NY: Doubleday.

Kelly, K., & Ramundo, P. (1993) <u>You mean I'm not lazy, stupid or crazy: A self-help book for adults with attention deficit disorder</u>. New York, NY: Scribner of Simon & Schuster, Inc.

Latham, P.S. & Latham, P.H. (1992) <u>Attention deficit disorder: A guide for advocates</u>. Washington, D.C.: JKL Communications.

Latham, P.S. & Latham, P.H. (1994) <u>Succeeding in the workplace: Attention deficit disorder and learning disabilities: A guide for success</u>. Washington, D.C.: JKL Communications.

Latham, P.S. & Latham, P.H. (1994) <u>Higher education services for learning disabilities and attention deficit disorder: A legal guide</u>. Washington, D.C.: JKL Communications.

Murphy, K.R., & Levert, S. (1995). <u>Out of the fog: Treatment options and coping strategies for adult attention deficit disorder</u>. New York, NY: Hyperion, Skylight Press Book.

Nadeau, K.G. (Ed.). (1995). <u>A comprehensive guide to attention deficit disorder in adults</u>. New York, NY: Brunner/Mazel Publishers.

Osman, B.B. (1982). <u>No one to play with: The social side of learning disabilities</u>. Novato, CA: Academic Therapy Publications.

Phelan, T.W. (1993). <u>All about attention deficit disorder: A comprehensive guide</u>. Glenn Ellyn, IL: Child Management, Inc.

Smith, S.L. (1992). <u>Succeeding against the odds: Strategies from the learning disabled</u>. Los Angeles, CA: Jeremy P. Tarcher, Inc.

Solden, S. (1995). <u>Women with attention deficit disorder: Embracing disorganization in the workplace</u>. Grass Valley, CA: Underwood Books.

Weiss, L. (1992). <u>Attention deficit disorders in adults</u>. Dallas, Texas: Taylor Publishing Company.

Weiss, L. (1994). <u>The attention deficit disorders in adults workbook</u>. Dallas, Texas: Taylor Publishing Company.

Whiteman, T.A., & Novotni, M. (1995). <u>Adult ADD: A reader-friendly guide to identifying, understanding, and treating adult attention deficit disorder</u>. Colorado Springs, CO: Pinon Press.

Recommended Learning Disabilities (LD) books

Adelizzi J.U., & Goss D.B. (1995). <u>A closer look: Perspective on college students with learning disabilities</u>. Milton, MA: Curry College.

Davis, R.D. (1994). <u>The gift of dyslexia: Why some of the smartest people can't read and how they can learn</u>. Burlington, CA: Ability Workshop Press.

Dennison, P.E. (1981). <u>Switching on: The whole brain answer to dyslexia.</u> Ventura, CA: Edu-Kinesthetics, Inc. (1-800-356-2109)

Houston, A.M. (1987). <u>Common sense about dyslexia</u>. New York, NY: Madison Books.

Latham, P.S., & Latham, P.H. (1992) <u>Learning disabilities and the law</u>. Washington, D.C.: JKL Communications. (202-223-5097)

Latham, P.S., & Latham, P.H. (1994) <u>Succeeding in the workplace: Attention deficit disorder and learning disabilities in the workplace: A guide for success</u>. Washington, D.C.: JKL Communications.

Latham, P.S. & Latham, P.H. (1994) <u>Higher education services for learning disabilities and attention deficit disorder: A legal guide</u>. Washington, D.C.: JKL Communications.

Lyman, D.E. (1994). <u>Making the words stand still: A master teacher tells how to overcome specific learning disabilities, dyslexia, and old-fashioned word blindness</u>. Boston, MA: Houghton Mifflin Company.

Nosek, K. (1995). <u>The dyslexic scholar</u>. Dallas Texas: Taylor Publishing.

Smith, S.L. (1991). <u>Succeeding against the odds: Strategies and insights from the learning disabled</u>. Los Angeles, CA: Jeremy P. Tarcher, Inc.

Recommended MBTI books

Myers-Briggs Type Indicator and MBTI are registered trademarks of Consulting Psychologists Press, Inc., Palo Alto, CA 94303.

DiTiberio, J.K., & Hammer, A.L. (1993). Introduction to type in college. Palo Alto, CA: Consulting Psychologists Press, Inc.

DiTiberio, J.K., & Jensen, G.H. (1995). Writing and personality: Finding your voice, your style, your way. Palo Alto, CA: Davies-Black Publishers.

Fairhurst, A.M., & Fairhurst, L.L. Effective teaching effective learning: Making the personality connection in your classroom. Palo Alto, CA: Davies-Black Publishing.

Hammer, A., & Macdaid, G.P. (1992). MBTI Career report manual. Palo Alto, CA: Consulting Psychologists Press, Inc.

Hammer, A. (1993). Introduction to type and careers. Palo Alto, CA: Consulting Psychologists Press, Inc.

Hirsh, S.K., & Kummerow, J.M. (1993). Introduction to type in organizations: Individual interpretive guide. Palo Alto, CA: Consulting Psychologists Press, Inc.

Isachsen, O., & Berens, L.V. (1988). Working together: A personality-centered approach to management. Coronado, CA: Neworld Management Press.

Keirsey, D., & Bates, M. (1984). Please understand me: Character and temperament types. Del Mar, CA: Prometheus Nemesis Book Company.

Kroeger, O. & Thuesen, J.M. (1988). Type talk: The 16 personality types that determine how we live, love, and work. New York, NY: Bantam Doubleday Dell Publishing Group, Inc.

Kroeger, O. & Thuesen, J.M. (1992). Type talk at work: How the 16 personality types determine your success on the job. New York, NY: Bantam Doubleday Dell Publishing Group, Inc.

Lawrence, G. (1993). People types and tiger stripes (3rd ed.). Gainesville, FL: Center for Applications of Psychological Type, Inc.

McCaulley M.H. (1989). <u>The Myers-Briggs Type Indicator and leadership</u>. Gainesville, FL: Center for Applications of Psychological Type, Inc. (800-777-2278)

Myers, I.B., & Myers, P.B. (1980). <u>Gifts differing: Understanding personality type</u>. Palo Alto, CA: Consulting Psychologists Press, Inc.

Myers, I.B., & McCaulley, M.H. (1985). <u>Manual: A guide to the development and use of the Myers-Briggs Type Indicator</u>. Palo Alto, CA: Consulting Psychologists Press, Inc.

Myers, I.B. (1974). <u>Type and teamwork</u>. Gainesville, FL: Center for Applications of Psychological Type, Inc.

Myers, I.B. (1993). <u>Introduction to type: A guide to understanding your results on the Myers-Briggs Type Indicator</u>. Palo Alto, CA: Consulting Psychologists Press, Inc.

Provost, J.A., & Anchors, S. (Editors). (1987). <u>Applications of the Myers-Briggs Type Indicator in higher education</u>. Palo Alto, CA: Consulting Psychologists Press, Inc.

Provost, J.A. (1988). <u>Procrastination: Using psychological type concepts to help students</u>. Gainesville, FL: Center for Applications of Psychological Type, Inc.

Saunders, F.W. (1991). <u>Katharine and Isabel: Mother's Light, Daughter's Journey</u>. Palo Alto, CA: Consulting Psychologists Press, Inc.

Silver, H.F., & Hanson, J.R. (1986). <u>Teaching styles and strategies</u>. Moorestown, NJ: Hanson Silver Strong & Associates, Inc.

VanSant, S., & Payne, D. (1995). <u>Psychological type in schools: Applications for educators</u>. Gainesville, FL: Center for Applications of Psychological Type, Inc.

Brain-based books

Amen, D.G. (1995). <u>Images into the mind: A radical new look at understanding and changing behavior.</u> Fairfield, CA: Mind Works Press. (707-429-7181)

Armstrong, T. (1993). <u>7 kinds of smart: Identifying and developing your many intelligences.</u> New York, NY: Penguin Books USA, Inc.

Bandler, R. (1985). <u>Using your brain for a change.</u> Moab, UT: Real People Press.

Buzan, T. (1977). <u>Make the most of your mind.</u> New York, NY: Simon & Schuster Inc.

Casebeer, B. (1981). <u>Using the right/left brain: An auditory imagery program.</u> Novato, CA: Academic Therapy Publications.

Covey, S.R. (1989). <u>The seven habits of highly effective people: Restoring the character ethic.</u> New York, NY: Simon & Schuster, Inc.

Dennison, G.E., Dennison, P.E. & Teplitz, J.V. (1995). <u>Brain gym for business: Instant brain boosters for on-the-job success.</u> Ventura, CA: Edu-Kinesthetics, Inc. (1-800-356-2109)

Dennison, P.E., & Dennison, G.E. (1989). <u>Brain gym: Teacher's edition revised.</u> Ventura, CA: Edu-Kinesthetics, Inc.

Dennison, P.E., & Dennison, G.E. (1995). <u>Edu-Kinesthetics in-depth; the seven dimensions of intelligence.</u> Ventura, CA: Edu-Kinesthetics, Inc.

Gardner, H. (1983). <u>Frames of mind: The theory of multiple intelligences.</u> New York, NY: Basic Books, Inc.

Gawain, S. (1982). <u>Creative visualization workbook: Use the power of your imagination to create what you want in life.</u> San Rafael, CA: New World Library.

Goleman, D. (1995). <u>Emotional intelligence.</u> New York: Bantam Books.

Grinder, M. (1991). <u>Righting the educational conveyor belt (2 ed.).</u> Portland, OR: Metamorphous Press.

Jensen, E. (1995). <u>Brain-based learning & teaching</u>. Del Mar, CA: Turning Point Publishing. (800-325-4769)

Lazear, D. (1991). <u>Seven ways of knowing: Understanding multiple intelligences</u>. Palatine, IL: Skylight Publishing, Inc.

Lyons, E.B. (1980). <u>How to use your power of visualization</u>. Red Bluff, CA: Lyons Visualization Series.

Matthews, A. (1988). <u>Being happy</u>. Los Angeles, CA: Price Stern Sloan, Inc.

Seligman, M.E.P. (1991). <u>Learned optimism</u>. New York, NY: Alfred A. Knopf, Inc.

Seligman, M.E.P. (1995). <u>The optimistic child</u>. New York, NY: Houghton Mifflin Company.

Sternberg, R.J. (1988). <u>The triarchic mind: A new theory of human intelligence</u>. New York, NY: Penguin Books USA, Inc.

Williams, R.H. & Stockmyer, J. (1987). <u>Unleashing the right side of the brain: The LARC creativity program</u>. Lexington, MA: The Stephen Greene Press.

Vail, P.L. (1981). <u>Emotion: The on/off switch for learning</u>. Rosemont, NJ: Modern Learning Press.

Videos about ADHD/ADD/LD

Amen, D.G. (1995). <u>Images into the mind: The Video</u>. Fairfield, CA: Mind Works Press (707-429-7181)

Barkley, R.A. (1992). <u>Video: ADHD - What do we know</u>? New York, NY: Guilford Publications, Inc.

Barkley, R.A. (1992). <u>Video: ADHD - What can we do</u>? New York, NY: Guilford Publications, Inc.

Barkley, R.A. (1994). <u>Video: ADHD in adults</u>. New York, NY: Guilford Publications, Inc.

Jensen, E. (1995). <u>Brain-based learning & teaching</u>.
P.O. Box 2251, Del Mar CA: Turning Point.
(800-325-4769)

Lavoie, R.D. (1989). <u>Video: How difficult can this be:
Understanding learning disabilities: The F.A.T. city
workshop</u>. Alexandria, VA: PBS.
(800-424-7963)

Lavoie, R.D. (1994). <u>Video: Learning disabilities and
social skills: Last one picked. . . first one picked on</u>.
Washington, D.C.: WETA Distributed by PBS.
(800-424-7963)

Organizations

ADDA - National Attention Deficit Disorder Association (ADDA) - An informational resource and advocate of support groups for both ADD adults and children. Subscription to newsletters and notification of workshops and conferences nation wide available. ADDA, P. O. Box 972, Mentor, OH 44061
(800-487-2282)

ADDult News - A quarterly newsletter for ADD adults. 2620 Ivey Place, Toledo, OH 43613
Compuserve U.I.D.# 75200,1463

ADDult Information Exchange Network - P. O. Box 1701, Ann Arbor, MI 48106

ADD-Vantage - Newsletter subscription information: P.O. Box 29972, Thornton, CO 80229-09672

ADDvisor - Attention Deficit Resource Center publication. P.O. Box 71223, Marietta, GA 30007-1223

Brain Gym - Educational Kinesiology Foundation P.O. Box 3396, Ventura, CA 93006-3396
(800-356-2109)

Children and Adults with Attention Deficit Disorders (CH.A.D.D.). A national organization that promotes support services for children, adults, and professionals interested in helping those with ADD. A national conference is sponsored annually. Membership includes newsletter, magazine, and notification of workshops and conferences offered around the country. CH.A.D.D. 499 N.W. 70th Avenue, Suite 109, Plantation, FL 33317
(305-587-3700)

Educational Kinesiology Foundation - Brain Gym publications and workshop information. P.O. Box 3396, Ventura, CA 93006-3396
(800-356-2109)

Learning Disibilities Association of America (LDA) - Membership to this organizations includes newsletters and notification of workshops and conferences regarding learning disabilities. There are also state chapters that address specific issues of that geographical area. LDA, 4156 Library Road, Pittsburgh, PA 15234
(412-341-1515)

Learning Disabilities Network - New England based educational and support services. 72 Sharp Street, Hingham, MA 02043
(617-340-5605)

MED-ADD Services - A pharmacotherapy consulting organization specializing in ADD, LD and related conditions. MED-ADD REVIEW is a newsletter of medication management available by subscription. Peter D. Anderson, Ph.D., Med-ADD Services, P.O. Box 252 Dorchester, MA 02124-2417
(617-287-1339)

National Coaching Network (NCN)- Those looking for an ADD coach can contact this organization to obtain a list of coaches in their geographical location. NCN, P.O. Box 353, Lafayette Hill, PA 19444
(610-825-8572)

National Attention Deficit Disorder Association (ADDA) - *see ADDA*

Rebus Institute - Topics of interest to adults with learning differences including ADD/ADHD/LD. 1499 Bayshore Blvd., Suite 146, Burlingame, CA 94010
(415-697-3734)

Distributors of books and videos

• **Academic Therapy Publishers** - Mail order catelog of books about learning issues and professional materials. 20 Commercial Boulevard, Novato, CA: 94949-6191
(800-422-7249)

• **A.D.D. Plus** - Mail order catelog of books and videos. 1095 25th Street SE, Suite 107, Salem, Oregon 97301 (800-847-1233)

• **A.D.D. Warehouse** - Mail order catelog of books and videos. 300 Northwest 70th Avenue, Suite 102, Plantation, FL 33317 (800-233-9273)

• **ADD Resources** - Books by mail, Consulting, Seminars, Conferences. 154 Curtis, Valpaiso, Indiana 46383 (800-409-4908)

• **Center for Applications of Plychological Type** - Catelog of Myers-Briggs Type Indicator (MBTI) books – CAPT, 2815 NW 13th Street, Suite 401, Gainesville, FL 32609 (800-777-2278)

• **Leadership Dimension Inc.** - Distributors of the MBTI Insight Game and other type/temperament materials. PO Box 424, Idyllwild, CA 92549 (909-659-4555)

• **Tuning Point** - "The Brain Store" mail order catelog of books and videos. 11080 Roselle St., Suite F, San Diego, CA 92121 (800-325-4769)

Appendix A

Additional Myers-Briggs Type Indicator (MBTI) Information

Note: Myers-Briggs Type Indicator and the MBTI are trademarks of the Consulting Psychological Press (CPP), Inc., Palo Alto, CA.

Myers-Briggs Type Indicator — Type Table

ISTJ	ISFJ	INFJ	INTJ
ISTP	ISFP	INFP	INTP
ESTP	ESFP	ENFP	INTP
ESTJ	ESFJ	ENFJ	ENTJ

The MBTI Device and Variations

The Myers-Briggs Type Indicator is a self-reporting device that was designed to help individuals understand themselves better. There are a number of variations of the Indicator itself. The most commonly administered one is the MBTI-Form G published by CPP. This consists of 94 statements that need to be responded to, honestly, for the results to be accurate. Upon completing the Indicator, it can be either self-scored or computer scored, depending upon the situation under which it was administered. Access to the MBTI-Form G is through qualified professionals who have been trained in its administration and interpretation. The MBTI is gaining popularity with career counselors, educational consultants and other professionals.

David Keirsey and Marilyn Bates (1984) have co-authored a book titled *Please Understand Me: Character & Temperament Types* based upon the 16 MBTI personality types. Included in this book is a self-administering and scoring inventory: The Keirsey Temperament Sorter. Keirsey's is one of many books that is listed in the Resource section of this book for those looking for additional information about the MBTI.

A variation of the MBTI is the "Insight Game" which is a card sorting of type preferences. This is available in both a board game and a computer game. The Insight Game is the registered trademark of and distributed by "The Leadership Dimension, Inc." in Louisville, Kentucky. Many people have responded favorably to the game form compared to the MBTI Form-G because of its non-intimidating nature.

Although taking the Form-G is not a "test," for many people it looks and feels like one. The sorting of cards with the Insight Game provides a more relaxed atmosphere. Results are obtained by counting each stack of sorted cards.

There are other inventories that have been developed to utilize MBTI information. As the MBTI popularity and applications expand, further alternatives for identifying "type" will most likely become available.

The 16 Personality Types of the MBTI

Extraversion (E)	vs	Introversion (I)
Sensing (S)	vs	iNtuitive (N)
Thinking (T)	vs	Feeling (F)
Judging (J)	vs	Perceiving (P)

ISTJ	ISFJ	INFJ	INTJ
ISTP	ISFP	INFP	INTP
ESTP	ESFP	ENFP	ENTP
ESTJ	ESFJ	ENFJ	ENTJ

Extraversion vs Introversion

In Myers-Briggs terms, Introversion and Extraversion refer to the preference for acquiring energy. Introverts become energized through self-reflection; Extraverts from interacting with the outside world.

This has strong implications in learning environments.

For example, introverted learners have a tendency to want to make sure they know the answer first, prior to offering a response. If asked a question, there may be a long pause as they search for an appropriate answer, and rehearse it in their minds. Educators who are not aware of this phenomenon often do not provide sufficient time for introverts to formulate their responses.

These learners may appear to be in their own world and not paying attention. Because of this, some introverted learners may incorrectly be labeled "slow learners." Extraverts have a tendency to speak before thinking through their answers. These learners process information by "talking it out." They may blurt out an answer before being called upon, and may find themselves being reprimanded for being impulsive.

By looking at the Introversion and Extraversion in this framework, they both could fall into the category of the ADHD/ADD-like behaviors. Introverts with distractibility and Extraverts with impulsivity. Looking at this as a preferred "style" of the brain, provides another framework for understanding differences and developing tolerances for differences. As mentioned in Chapter 4, we all have ADHD/ADD experiences at sometime in our lives. One way to decide if an ADHD/ADD assessment is appropriate is to consider the "degree" and "frequency" of these interferences and whether they have been preventing accomplishment of life goals. Remember, there is a wide range of "normal". The MBTI was developed specifically for normal people as a self-help device. It is a wonderful tool to help understand differences among individuals and to celebrate the gifts that their particular type brings with it.

Extravert (E)
- Prefers to **talk** out the problem
- Easily **verbally expresses** ideas, thoughts, and feelings
- Brainstorms **out loud**
- **Discusses** advantages and disadvantages of possible solutions
- Likes to **be with others**
- Likes to be able to **move around,** rather than sitting in one place

Introvert (I)
- Needs **time** to reflect before responding
- May prefer to respond in **writing** rather than verbally
- Prefers to **think** about possible options **before sharing** them with others
- Prefers to work **independently**
- Others may have to ask for their ideas, thoughts and feelings

Sensing (S) vs iNtuitive (N)
Sensing (S) types prefer to acquire information through the 5 senses (touch, taste, smell, hear, see). As learners, they like to be actively involved with the content they are learning. They want to experience as much as they can about the topic. They like to move

around, being kinesthetically oriented.

Classrooms are usually very "sensing" oriented through the primary grades, and become more lecture oriented from 4th grade on. This places the learners with a Sensing (S) preference at a disadvantage in the classroom compared to the Intuitive (N) types.

The preference for acquiring information for the Intuitive (N) types is with the 6th sense. They may have a more positive learning experience in a lecture type classroom, but their disadvantage is seeing the "big picture" without the specific details.

The Sensing (S) types have a better knack for grasping the details, but have a more difficult time with the big picture.

From an ADHD/ADD perspective, some Sensing (S) types may be too kinesthetic for the traditional classroom setting, not being able to sit still in their seats, and wanting to touch everything.

Intuitive (N) types can sometimes escape too much into a world of possibilities and not be in touch with the reality of the lesson being presented.

Once again, as cautioned with the Extravert (E) and Introvert (I), question whether this is a disability or just a styles preference of the brain. It is a matter of degree and whether or not life goals are being actualized because of the amount of movement and the need to touch. Or having so many ideas that a person can not focus on one idea long enough to determine its practicality or application.

Sensing (S)
- **Looks** at the facts that are currently present
- Usually follows policy and guidelines
- Seeks **practical,** realistic **solutions**
- Likes information presented clearly and concisely, gets to the bottom line
- **Prefers step-by-step** progressions (likes outlines)
- May be **detail** oriented

Intuitive (N)

- Perceives things in a **broad spectrum,** looking beyond immediate facts
- Looks for **possibilities,** interconnections, implications and patterns
- Looks for ways to prevent reoccurrences of the situation
- Seeks solutions that have **long-range** impact
- Seeks solutions that are **creative, innovative,** future-oriented
- Sees the **"big picture"** – sometimes gets lost in details
- Likes variety
- Prefers to work at their **own pace**

Thinking (T) vs Feeling (F)

Thinking (T) preference for decision making looks at options objectively. Only the facts relevant to the situation are considered.

A Feeling (F) preference implies that decisions are made depending upon the situation. A subjective approach is taken. Thinking types sometimes may think that Feeling types take things too personally. Feeling (F) types sometimes may feel that Thinking types do not take into consideration the "people" factor when making decisions.

ADHD/ADD characteristics are more like those of the Feeling (F) types while the ADHD/ADDers may have a tendency to jump to conclusions without thoroughly seeking the facts. Remember, no type is better than another. It is not good, it is not bad, it just is. Understanding how people learn, process and interpret information can help improve the chances of effective communications.

Thinking (T)

- Makes **decisions** impersonally based on the **facts**
- Rational and logical in going about seeking solutions

- Values fairness and consistency
- Seeks solutions that will get at the cause of the situation
- Tries hard not to personalize the situation, staying focussed on the task
- Likes to **debate** facts
- May ask **"why"** questions
- Prefers **information** presented to be **fast-paced**

Feeling (F)

- Places higher value on **personal** concerns of those involved rather than data analysis
- Likes to involve others in the decision making process
- Values **harmony** and seeks **consensus**
- Seeks to find solutions that everyone can agree with
- Begins problem solving by identifying parts everyone agrees with first

Judging (J) vs Perceiving (P)

Judging (J) and Perceiving (P) describes the preference for type of life-style. The Judging types, as in judicious, prefer structure; everything has a place with everything in its place. They generally do not like surprises in terms of scheduling changes. Perceiving types prefer spontaneity. Too much scheduling may cramp their style.

The Perceiving type may have ADHD/ADD characteristics. Especially significant is a tendency to have difficulty following through with projects. Many Perceiving types become excited about a project and start with much enthusiasm and energy. As the project becomes more routine, and possibly more time consuming than anticipated, interest may begin to wane. Once again, does that make all Perceiving types ADHD/ADD? No! The degree of ADHD/ADD characteristics that appear to get in the way of self-actualization is the determining factor.

Judging (J)
- Seeks **closure** in a relatively **short time-span**
- Prefers a **quick** resolution
- Likes **predictability**
- Prefers to know expectations up front

Perceiving (P)
- Seeks to keep **options open**
- No need for quick solutions
- Likes **choices**
- Prefers **flexibility**

Remember, the dynamics of typology go beyond these eight letter descriptions (I/E, S/N, T/F, J/P). The interaction between the four letters that make up the 16 personality types create another dimension. Refer to Chapter 3 for a brief narrative of each of the types.

The Resource section of this book contains a list of references for further inquiry into the MBTI.

Appendix B

More about Emotional Intelligence

The two parts of the brain that are being attributed to Emotional Intelligence (EQ) are the limpic system (middle or mammilian brain) and the neocortex (new brain).

We need emotions to give us quality to our lives, such as empathy, happiness, sadness, self-reflection. The neocortex, or thinking part of the brain, provides us with rational decision making and reasoning. A balance between "thinking" and "feeling" are needed in order for us to experience our full potential.

The limpic system houses the emotions. This is where the "fight or flight syndrome" occurs. It makes instantanous decisions. Depending upon our "style" of handling fearful or angry situations, we may have a tendency to either want to run away from the sitatuion (flight) or to lash out in defense (fight). Although these are instinctional responses, they are not always appropriate by today's civilized standards. As discussed in Chapter 5, in the beginning of human evolutional the emotional brain provided quick responses to danger: "kill or be killed."

The neocortex is the thinking part of the brain. Compared to the emotional brain, it processes information much more slowly. It organizes and categories facts in a thoughtful, judicial manner. The thinking brain can be utilized as the "off switch" when our emotions begin to run amuck. Our best intentions to be conscientious and responsible can be sabotaged by an emotional experience.

Although some people may appear to have been born with natural EQ ability, it is something that we can all develop. It will take time, commitment, and a lot of self-reflection. Balance is the objective. Both the limpic system and the neocortex are of equal importance.

Research indicates that EQ has more of an impact on the ability to "succeed" than intelligence. It takes more than being smart to navigate through life. The ability to communicate effectively with people, to be able to read non-verbal communication, requires EQ. More is said through body language, intonations and eye movement than the spoken word. To be aware of these is being aware of yourself. The ability to respond to others, empathetically, requires effective use of the limpic system. To hold a rational conversation and set priorities require effective use of the neocortex. Combining these two provide for humane and productive communications.

Appendix C

What works for me!

The following are examples of strategies that have helped me in coping with and compensating for my LDness and ADDness. They are provided as concrete explanations of some of the more philosophical concepts presented in this book. What follows are brain-based, brain-compatible activities that are right/left brained, mind/body, visual, kinesthetic, and free flowing.

These are just a few examples. If you are interested, try some or all of them. If they work, great. If you are so inclined, tinker with them. Adjust, adapt, or modify them to make them work for you. Take what works and leave the rest!

ADHD/ADD/LD manifest themselves differently in those who experience them. Therefore, strategies need to be developed or fine-tuned to meet individual needs. Think of this as an adventure in getting to know yourself better. Have fun with it!

Energy Levels

This is a free flowing drawing of shapes, colors, and lines. The idea is to take a piece of paper and begin drawing. No need for a plan. You can draw objects such as trees, flowers, cars, houses, scenery; or doodle, draw designs or scribble. This can be done with

any medium: crayons, markers, craypods, pen, pencil, etc. It only takes a few minutes to draw one. No need to worry, you can not do this wrong! It is whatever you make of it. For those who want to collect their pictures in an orderly manner, a drawing pad is suggested. What you may want to do is date them as I do. It can be fun to look back at these to see what patterns evolve.

Purpose: to release energy and to shift your state of mind. This is very much a right brained experience. It is a good activity when "stuck" and wanting or needing to shift gears. Example: An error in the checkbook can not be found (a left-brain activity). Take a few minutes to do an Energy Level activity. Now, try completing the left-brained task. Did it help?

Visualizing the Outcome, First

When I do not know where to begin a project or assignment, I find it helpful to visualize what I want it to look like when it is finished. This helps me see the "big picture."

Having a preference for processing information "whole-to-parts," I need to see the "whole" so that I can begin the process of identifying the "parts" or steps that need to be taken in order to accomplish the task. This backwards approach allows me to "see" what needs to be done.

An example of this is developing a presentation or workshop. The first step is to identify "what" I want the audience to "walk away with" at the end of the presentation. I visualize the arrangement of the room, the number of people, the time of day, the length of the presentation. I envision the posters or visual aids that will be helpful to reinforce the "bottom line."

Once this has been accomplished, the next step is to determine the actual "teachable time" available. I deduct "futz time" and breaks. Futz time is time lost at the very beginning of the session, settling down after breaks, and when there are break-out groups, allowing a minute or two for breaking up and getting back to the whole group setting again. A five hour workshop adjusted for breaks and futz time usually results in a four-and-a-quarter hour workshop. I reality-test the "bottom line" to ensure that this will be enough time to reach the desired goal.

Next, I determine the subtopics that will lead up to the "bottom line." Once these have been identified, I visualize the activities that will reinforce the ideas presented. I keep the size of room and the number of people in my mind as I try to decide what will be "doable" in the space and time available. This process continues until the lesson plans, handouts, training aids, and the like are established.

Treats

It is important for me to give myself little rewards along the way. Even if I don't complete the entire task, I look to see what piece(s) were completed and congratulate myself for them. Example of treats:

- long, hot bubble bath with calming music and candles (and my husband when he is available)
- hot pot of my favorite tea
- reading for pleasure – My husband and I like to read to each other at night to "wind down"
- buying a used video for $5.00 at the local video store
- going for a walk

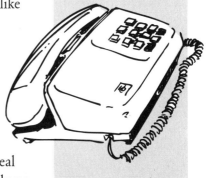

The phone

I work at home a lot. The phone can be a real distractor! I turn the answering machine on, volume off, and bell tone off. The message on the tape says that I am "not available," not that I am "not home" – so I am not even lying!

Finding a special place in a hectic schedule

One of my favorite views is Nantasket Beach, Hull, Massachusetts. I frequently have consulting opportunities in this town and I try to schedule myself to arrive early so I have a few minutes to "chill out." No matter what the weather, the scenery is always spectacular overlooking Massachusetts Bay and the Atlantic Ocean. Three lighthouses can be seen from this one location: Boston Light, Minots Light, and Graves Light. On calm days the ocean is tranquil, while other days the seas can be whipping up in fury.

It reminds me so much of myself; sometimes feeling calm and at peace, and other times in a whirlwind of intensity. Regardless of the weather, season or sea conditions, I always find it comforting to watch the ocean blend into the sky on the horizon. When I arrive at my destination, I feel in control and energized.

PMS

Dealing with my menstrual cycle has been challenging. I find it helpful to attempt to realistically schedule my life for the week prior to my period. I find that I tend to drive more recklessly, am more easily driven to distraction, and be less patient during this critical time. Consequently, I try to limit the distance I have to travel, preferably to work at home or within a few miles of home.

I also make a conscious effort to reduce the number of tasks that need to be completed during this time. I have a tendency to become very disorganized and unable to find things.

Conversely, this is also the time when I become most creative, so burning the midnight oil until the wee hours of the morning is common. This is okay when I can sleep during the day; but it can create problems when I have a very busy day ahead of me. Rather than getting angry and berating myself during this period, I work at creative scheduling.

Conclusion

I give myself permission to do things differently and do things that work for me! I have always marched to the beat of a different drummer, and now I know that it's okay to do so.

If a man does not keep pace with his companions, perhaps it is because he hears a different drummer. Let him step to the music which he hears, however measured or far away.
• **Henry David Thoreau**

Glossary

ADHD/ADD - Attention Deficit-Hyperactivity Disorders

ADD Coach - a professional who works with ADD adults to help them establish structure, skills and strategies to their lives; one-on-one contracted service

Americans with Disabilities Act - legislation requiring accommodations for those with disabilities including ADHD/ADD/LD

Brain-Based - a philosophy that refers to providing brain-compatible learning experiences; includes body-mind integration such as with Brain-Gym and the multiple intelligence

Brain-Gym - a whole-brain experience for enhancing the brain's ability to function through low-impact body movement; Educational Kinesiology developed by Dr. Paul E. Dennison

Classroom Trauma - an emotional shock created by past negative schooling experiences causing psychological difficulties interfering with academic success

Comobility - having more than one medical diagnosis (ex: depression and ADD)

Continuum - in reference to ADHD/ADD characteristics: a line with one end representing no ADHD/ADD characteristics, with the other end representing the ultimate extreme of experiencing ADHD/ADD characteristics

No ADHD/ADD   Extreme ADHD/ADD

Edu-Kinesthetic - see Brain-Gym

Emotional Intelligence (EQ) – the ability to effectively manage our emotions to enable us to develop to our fullest potential (self-actualize).

Helplessness - the inability to know how to help yourself

Hyper-focus - concentrating to the maximum, not allowing for any disruptions; a strategy used by many ADHD/ADD/LDers

Jung, Dr. Carl - the psychologist from Switzerland that developed the theory of psychological type (typology) that the Myers-Briggs Type Indicator (MBTI) is based upon.

Learning Disabilities (LD) - There are over 48 recognized definitions in the US. The one described by the DSM-IV is: "characterized by academic functioning that is substantially below that expected given the person's chronological age, measured intelligence, and age-appropriate education." These include reading, math, written expression, and "otherwise not specified" (DSM-IV, 1994, p. 38). A report presented by the Interagency Committee on Learning Disabilities in 1987 "defined to include: specific developmental disabilities of reading, writing, and mathematics, developmental language disorders, social skills deficits, and attention deficit disorder" (Latham & Latham, 1994, p. 28).

Metacognative Awareness - knowing how you, personally, gain knowledge (learn); self-knowledge of how information is acquired and processed

Multiple Intelligence - Dr. Howard Gardner's theory that there are at least 7 different types of intelligences: logical/mathematical, verbal/linguistic,

visual/spatial, body/kinesthetic, musical/
rhythmic, interpersonal, and intrapersonal

Myers-Briggs Type Indicator (MBTI) - an inventory based upon Dr. Carl Jung's work with psychological type. The Indicator was developed by a mother-daughter team, Isabel Myers and Katharine Briggs.

NeuroLinguistic Programming (NLP) - developed by Dr. Richard Bandler in the 1970's to maximize human learning potential; it is a process in consciously deciding what it is you want out of life, identifying things that are interfering with achieving it, and doing something about; it is process for taking control of your own life

Neuro-Psychological Evaluation (Assessment) - a battery of standardized tests given to a person to determine how their brain functions

Paradigm - an ideal, pattern or model

Parts-to-Whole - preferring "details" presented sequentially ordered, first, building up to the "big picture"

Psycho-Educational Assessment (Evaluation) - a battery of tests given to a person to determine their learning potential

Self-Actualize - to realize your full potential; to achieve the ultimate self-directed life goal

SPECT - Single Photon Emission Computerized Tomography - a color coded electronic mapping of the brain's activity (Dr. Daniel Amen is noted for his research in this area)

Styles - each individual possess a unique manner (style) of taking in and processing information

Third-Eye or the Mind's Eye - refers to where "visualizations" occur. This is located in the middle of the forehead. When asked to close your eyes and "picture" something, this is where the mind displays it.

Typology - the study of personality or psychological types used by the Myers-Briggs Type Indicator (MBTI)

VAKT - refers to a preference for acquiring and processing information through **V**isual, **A**uditory, **K**inesthetic or **T**actile manner

Whole-Brain Theory - to use the brain to its fullest potential; using the left and right halves of the brain (hemispheres) to optimize learning experiences; integrating the mind and body to seek balance

Whole-to-Parts - preferring the "big picture", first and then determining where the parts (details) fit in

Index

Notes . . .